CATHOLIC
ALL
DECEMBER

Catholic All December

Traditional Catholic prayers, Bible passages, songs, and devotions for the month of the Immaculate Conception

A COMPANION TO
THE CATHOLIC ALL YEAR COMPENDIUM

Kendra Tierney

The text of these traditional prayers are in the public domain. Newer prayers are cited where possible.

Illustrations are from various editions of the Roman Missal that are out of copyright, and other vintage books similarly out of copyright.

Scripture texts in this work are taken from the New American Bible with Revised New Testament and Revised Psalms © 1991, 1986, 1970 Confraternity of Christian Doctrine, Washington, D.C. and are used by permission of the copyright owner. All Rights Reserved. No part of the New American Bible may be reproduced in any form without permission in writing from the copyright owner.

Some prayers from the *Book of Blessings* Prepared by the International Commission on English in the Liturgy A Joint Commission of Catholic Bishops' Conferences, The Liturgical Press, Collegeville, Minnesota. 1989

Prayer to Saint Nicholas from *Santa's Secret Story* by Cornelia Mary Bilinsky, 2009, Pauline Books & Media.

Information on indulgences is from *Manual of Indulgences: Norms and Grants*, Apostolic Penitentiary, Washington, D.C., United States Conference of Catholic Bishops, 2006.

Papal prayers and encyclicals from Vatican.va

This compilation is copyright Kendra Tierney 2019, all rights reserved..

For more liturgical living ideas, check out www.CatholicAllYear.com and *The Catholic All Year Compendium*, available wherever books are sold.

This booklet is available as a paperback at www.Amazon.com ISBN: 9781688421547 and as a printable pdf at www.CatholicAllYear.com

ALSO BY KENDRA TIERNEY:

Monthly Prayer Booklets for each month
January-December
Catholic All Year Stations of the Cross Booklet
A Visit to the Blessed Sacrament Booklet
Catholic All Day Daily Prayer Booklet
Christmas Novena Booklet
Catholic All Year Hymns and Carols for Advent
and Christmas
*the above are available as printable pdfs at www.CatholicAllYear.com
or as paperback booklets at www.Amazon.com*

Catholic All Year Printable Lent featuring a
Lent Countdown Calendar, Voluntary Lenten
Discipline commitment slips, and a Lenten
Sacrifice Bean Jar label

Investiture in the Brown Scapular Booklet
Rosary of the Seven Sorrows Booklet
Seven Sorrows Scripture Activity Booklet
May Crowning Booklet
Divine Mercy Novena Booklet
13 Month Liturgical Year Wall Calendar
Advent Wreath Prayers Booklet
At Home Nativity Play Booklet

A Little Book About Confession for Children
My Superhero Prayer Book
My Fairy-Tale Prayer Book
My Woodland Prayer Book
The Catholic All Year Compendium
find them all at www.CatholicAllYear.com

User guide

Don't stress and don't think you have to do it all!

In this booklet, you'll find all the Bible passages, prayers, songs, and devotions for this month that our family uses to enhance our family prayer life and our liturgical living in the home. These are the prayers and practices that I recommend in my book, *The Catholic All Year Compendium*. There wasn't room in what was already a very long book to include all of them in the text, and they're all available right there on our phones.

Still, I don't know about you, but I really prefer paper over screens when I'm praying. I could blame it on the distractibility of my kids, but . . . I'm also pretty distractible. So, my plan is to create twelve of these booklets, one for each month. I'll keep them close at hand, for easy, screen-free access to the prayers, etc. that we like to use on various feast days. For all the history, tradition, and backstories surrounding these devotions and the feast days to which they are attached, please consult the book.

We try to work these prayers into our days in a way that doesn't add to our stress and busyness. We add a short prayer to the end of our grace before meals for the month, to help us stay mindful of the recommended devotion, and we add special litanies, prayers, and songs to our evening prayers as often as we are able, always depending on the circumstances of the day, week, year.

Many of these prayers are associated with indulgences, either partial or plenary (full), pursuant to the usual conditions. The Collect Prayers included come from that feast day's Mass propers, and a partial indulgence is available for the use of those prayers. See Appendix B of *The Catholic All Year Compendium* for a thorough explanation of indulgences.

V̄ and R̄ in the text refer to "versicle" which is the leader's part, and "response" for everyone else.

Family 3 Special Days this month

BIRTHDAYS, NAMEDAYS, BAPTISM ANNIVERSARIES

Table of Contents

Letter From the Author	10
Grace + Christmas Anticipation Prayer	11
ADVENT WREATH BLESSING & PRAYERS	12
Immaculate Conception Novena	18
December 6—Saint Nicholas	20
The Nicene Creed	21
December 7—Saint Ambrose	22
December 8—Immaculate Conception	23
Renewal of Consecration of the US	24
December 9—Saint Juan Diego	25
December 10—Our Lady of Loreto	26
Litany of Loreto	27
December 12—Our Lady of Guadalupe	29
December 13—Saint Lucy	31
This Little Light of Mine	32
December 14—Saint John of the Cross	33
CHRISTMAS NOVENA	35
Magnificat	70
Gaudete Sunday/Bambinelli Sunday	72
Blessing of a Manger or Nativity Scene	73
December 24—Christmas Eve/Saints Adam & Eve	74
Blessing & Lighting of a Christmas Tree	80
Prayer Before Baby Jesus in the Manger	82
Hymns: Silent Night/Away in a Manger	83

84	December 25—Christmas/the Nativity of the Lord
86	AN AT HOME NATIVITY PLAY SCRIPT
96	December 26—Saint Stephen
98	Prayer for Deacons and other Ministers
99	Hymn: Good King Wenceslas
100	December 27—Saint John, Apostle & Evangelist
102	Blessing of Wine/Drinking the Love of Saint John
103	Prayers for Priests
104	December 28—The Holy Innocents
105	Altar Server's Prayer
107	Hymn: Coventry Carol
108	Feast of the Holy Family
110	SONGS FOR ADVENT
111	Come Thou Long Expected Jesus
	Lo! How a Rose E're Blooming
112	O Come O Come Emmanuel
113	Veni, Veni Emmanuel
114	Creator Alme Siderum
115	Creator of the Stars of Night
116	O Come Divine Messiah
117	Let All Mortal Flesh Keep Silence
118	The Angel Gabriel from Heaven Came
119	People Look East
120	I'll Be Home for Christmas
	Christmas Is Coming
121	Silver Bells
122	Santa Claus is Coming to Town
123	Deck the Halls
	Jingle Bells
124	SONGS FOR CHRISTMAS
125	I Saw Three Ships Come Sailing In
126	Children Go Where I Send Thee
127	Angels We Have Heard on High
128	What Child Is This?
	Joy to the World
129	Hark, the Herald Angels Sing
130	O Come All Ye Faithful
	Adeste Fideles
131	O Little Town of Bethlehem
	The First Noel
132	God Rest Ye Merry Gentlemen
	We Wish you a Merry Christmas
133	We Three Kings
134	The Twelve Days of Christmas

Dear Reader,

Advent and the new Catholic liturgical year begin on the Sunday closest to the feast of St. Andrew on November 30, which, despite what every Advent calendar thinks, is rarely on December 1. So you'll find pre-Advent prayers, and instructions for making an Advent wreath in the Catholic All November Booklet.

This booklet includes everything you'll need for a prayerful Advent and beginning of the Christmas season, including the Christmas Anticipation Prayer, the Immaculate Conception Novena, weekly Advent wreath prayers, the Christmas Novena, an order for the at home blessing of a manger or nativity scene, a Christmas tree, and wine, and an At Home Nativity Play script.

You'll also find prayers, devotions, Bible readings, songs, poems, and historical documents for Advent and Christmas saints including Saint Nicholas, Saint Ambrose, Saint Juan Diego, Our Lady of Loreto, Our Lady of Guadalupe, Saint Lucy, Saint John of the Cross, Saints Adam and Eve, Saint Stephen, the Holy Innocents, and the Holy Family.

Also included are hymns and carols appropriate for the preparation for and celebration of the Christmas season.

The month of December is dedicated to Our Lady, Immaculately Conceived, as is the United States of America. In honor of her feast day on December 8, you'll find prayers including a renewal of the consecration to the Immaculate Conception.

It's a busy time of year, so be sure to choose the prayers, devotions, and activities that work for your family, schedule, season of life, and temperament. You don't have to do it all!

By the light of the incarnation,

Kendra Tierney
Kendra Tierney, 2019

December: dedicated to the Immaculate Conception

GRACE BEFORE MEALS
Bless us, O Lord, and these thy gifts, which we are about to receive, from thy bounty, through Christ, Our Lord, Amen.

THE CHRISTMAS ANTICIPATION PRAYER
Hail and blessed be the hour and moment, In which the Son of God was born of the most pure Virgin Mary at midnight, in Bethlehem, in the piercing cold. In that hour vouchsafe, I beseech Thee, O my God, to hear my prayer and grant my desires, through the merits of Our Savior Jesus Christ and of His blessed Mother. Amen.

MIRACULOUS MEDAL PRAYER
O Mary, conceived without sin, pray for us who have recourse to thee. Amen.

Advent Wreath Prayers

The blessing of the wreath

The Saturday before the first Sunday of Advent is Catholic New Year's Eve! It's customary on this day to make or set up the Advent wreath, and then, at the evening meal, to bless it. We also like to have a champange/sparking cider toast to the new liturgical year!

LEADER: Our help is in the name of the Lord.

ALL: Who made heaven and earth.

LEADER: O God, by whose Word all things are sanctified, pour forth Your blessing upon this wreath and grant that we who use it may prepare our hearts for the coming of Christ and may receive from You abundant graces. We ask this through Christ our Lord.

ALL: Amen.

Then the wreath (and everyone in the splash zone) gets sprinkled with holy water, if you have some handy. Many parishes have a holy water dispenser in the church, just bring your own container. If you're not sure how to get some, just ask your priest, or someone in the parish office.

First week of Advent

LEADER: O Lord, stir up Thy might, we beg Thee, and come, That by Thy protection we may deserve to be rescued from the threatening dangers of our sins and saved by Thy deliverance. Through Christ our Lord.

ALL: Amen.

Light the first purple candle. Let it burn during the meal.

Second week of Advent

LEADER: O Lord, stir up our hearts that we may prepare for Thy only begotten Son, that through His coming we may be made worthy to serve Thee with pure minds. Through Christ our Lord.

ALL: Amen.

Light the first and second purple candles. Let them burn during the meal.

Third week of Advent

LEADER: O Lord, we beg Thee, incline Thy ear to our prayers and enlighten the darkness of our minds by the grace of Thy visitation. Through Christ our Lord.

ALL: Amen.

Light the first and second purple candles, and the pink candle. Let them burn during the meal.

Fourth week of Advent

LEADER: O Lord, stir up Thy power, we pray Thee, and come; and with great might help us, that with the help of Thy Grace, Thy merciful forgiveness may hasten what our sins impede. Through Christ our Lord.

ALL: Amen.

Light all four candles. Let them burn during the meal.

Immaculate Conception Novena

The Feast of the Immaculate Conception is December 9. In preparation, this novena is prayed once a day from November 30 - December 8.

Immaculate Virgin! Mary, conceived without sin! Remember, you were miraculously preserved from even the shadow of sin, because you were destined to become not only the Mother of God, but also the mother, the refuge, and the advocate of man; penetrated therefore, with the most lively confidence in your never-failing intercession, we most humbly implore you to look with favor upon the intentions of this novena, and to obtain for us the graces and the favors we request.

You know, O Mary, how often our hearts are the sanctuaries of God, who abhors iniquity. Obtain for us, then, that angelic purity which was your favorite virtue, that purity of heart which will attach us to God alone, and that purity of intention which will consecrate every thought, word, and action to his greater glory. Obtain also for us a constant spirit of prayer and self-denial, that we may recover by penance that innocence which we have lost by sin, and at length attain safely to that blessed abode of the saints, where nothing defiled can enter.

O Mary, conceived without sin, pray for us who have recourse to you.
V. You are all fair, O Mary. R. You are all fair, O Mary.
V. And the original stain is not in you.
R. And the original stain is not in you.
V. You are the glory of Jerusalem.
R. You are the joy of Israel.
V. You are the honor of our people.
R. You are the advocate of sinners.
V. O Mary, Virgin, most prudent
R. O Mary, Mother, most tender.
V. Pray for us. R. Intercede for us with Jesus our Lord.

℣. In your conception, Holy Virgin, you were immaculate.
℟. Pray for us to the Father whose Son you brought forth.
℣. O Lady! aid my prayer.
℟. And let my cry come unto you.
Let us pray, Holy Mary, Queen of Heaven, Mother of Our Lord Jesus Christ, and mistress of the world, who forsakes no one, and despises no one, look upon me, O Lady! with an eye of pity, and entreat for me of your beloved Son the forgiveness of all my sins; that, as I now celebrate, with devout affection, your holy and immaculate conception, so, hereafter I may receive the prize of eternal blessedness, by the grace of him whom you, in virginity, did bring forth, Jesus Christ Our Lord: who, with the Father and the Holy Ghost, lives and reigns, in perfect Trinity, God, world without end. Amen.

Saint Nicholas

DECEMBER 6TH OPTIONAL MEMORIAL

COLLECT PRAYER
We humbly implore your mercy, Lord: protect us in all dangers through the prayers of the Bishop Saint Nicholas, that the way of salvation may lie open before us. Through our Lord Jesus Christ, your Son, who lives and reigns with you in the unity of the Holy Spirit, one God, for ever and ever. Amen.

PRAYER TO SAINT NICHOLAS

Saint Nicholas, faithful disciple of Jesus Christ, pray for us.
Saint Nicholas, example of Christian love, pray for us.
Saint Nicholas, helper of the poor and needy, pray for us.
Saint Nicholas, champion of orphans and widows, pray for us.
Saint Nicholas, protector of those who sail at sea, pray for us.
Saint Nicholas, defender of the true faith, pray for us.
Saint Nicholas, patron of children around the world, pray for us.
Saint Nicholas, secret giver of gifts, pray for us.
Saint Nicholas, the great wonderworker, pray for us.
Saint Nicholas, our friend in Heaven,
pray for us.
Amen.

THE NICENE CREED

I believe in one God,
the Father almighty,
maker of heaven
and earth,
of all things visible
and invisible.

I believe in one Lord
Jesus Christ,
the Only Begotten
Son of God,
born of the Father
before all ages.
God from God,
Light from Light,
true God from
true God,
begotten, not made, consubstantial with the Father;
through him all things were made.
For us men and for our salvation
he came down from heaven,
and by the Holy Spirit was incarnate of the Virgin
Mary,
and became man.
For our sake he was crucified under Pontius Pilate,
he suffered death and was buried,
and rose again on the third day
in accordance with the Scriptures.
He ascended into heaven
and is seated at the right hand of the Father.
He will come again in glory
to judge the living and the dead
and his kingdom will have no end.

I believe in the Holy Spirit, the Lord, the giver of life,
who proceeds from the Father and the Son,
who with the Father and the Son is adored and
glorified,
who has spoken through the prophets.

I believe in one, holy, catholic and apostolic Church.
I confess one Baptism for the forgiveness of sins
and I look forward to the resurrection of the dead
and the life of the world to come. Amen.

Saint Ambrose

DECEMBER 7TH MEMORIAL

COLLECT PRAYER

O God, who made the Bishop Saint Ambrose a teacher of the Catholic faith and a model of apostolic courage, raise up in your Church men after your own heart to govern her with courage and wisdom. Through our Lord Jesus Christ, your Son, who lives and reigns with you in the unity of the Holy Spirit, one God, for ever and ever. Amen.

PENITENTIAL PRAYER OF SAINT AMBROSE OF MILAN

O Lord, who has mercy upon all, take away from me my sins, and mercifully kindle in me the fire of your Holy Spirit. Take away from me the heart of stone, and give me a heart of flesh, a heart to love and adore you, a heart to delight in you, to follow and enjoy you, for Christ's sake, Amen

BLESSING OF BEES

O Lord, God almighty, who has created heaven and earth and every animal existing over them and in them for the use of men, and who has commanded through the ministers of holy Church that candles made from the products of bees be lit in church during the carrying out of the sacred office in which the most holy Body and Blood of Jesus Christ your Son is made present and is received; may your holy blessing descend upon these bees and these hives, so that they may multiply, be fruitful and be preserved from all ills and that the fruits coming forth from them may be distributed for your praise and that of your Son and the holy Spirit and of the most blessed Virgin Mary. Amen.

The Immaculate Conception of the Blessed Virgin Mary

DECEMBER 8TH SOLEMNITY/HOLY DAY OF OBLIGATION

COLLECT PRAYER

O God, who by the Immaculate Conception of the Blessed Virgin prepared a worthy dwelling for your Son, grant, we pray, that, as you preserved her from every stain by virtue of the Death of your Son, which you foresaw, so, through her intercession, we, too, may be cleansed and admitted to your presence. Through our Lord Jesus Christ, your Son, who lives and reigns with you in the unity of the Holy Spirit, one God, for ever and ever.

PRAYER ON THE SOLEMNITY OF THE IMMACULATE CONCEPTION

Father, the image of the Virgin is found in your Church.
Mary had a faith that your Spirit prepared and a love that never knew sin,
for you kept her sinless from the first moment of her conception.
Trace in our actions the lines of her love, in our hearts her readiness of faith.
Prepare once again a world for your Son who lives and reigns with you and the Holy Spirit, one God, forever and ever.

-Catholic Household Blessings and Prayers

PRAYER FOR RENEWAL OF CONSECRATION OF THE UNITED STATES TO ITS PATRONESS, THE IMMACULATE CONCEPTION

Most holy trinity: Our Father in heaven, who chose Mary as the fairest of your daughters; Holy Spirit, who chose Mary as your spouse; God the son, who chose Mary as your mother; in union with Mary, we adore your majesty and acknowledge your supreme, eternal dominion and authority.

Most Holy Trinity, we put the United States of America into the hands of Mary immaculate in order that she may present the country to you. Through her we wish to thank you for the great resources of this land and for the freedom, which has been its heritage.

Through the intercession of Mary, have mercy on the Catholic Church in America. Grant us peace. Have mercy on our president and on all the officers of our government. Grant us a fruitful economy born of justice and charity. Have mercy on capital and industry and labor. Protect the family life of the nation. Guard the precious gift of many religious vocations. Through the intercession of our mother, have mercy on the sick, the poor, the tempted, sinners – on all who are in need.

Mary, immaculate virgin, our mother, patroness of our land, we praise you and honor you and give our country and ourselves to your sorrowful and immaculate heart. O sorrowful and immaculate heart of Mary pierced by the sword of sorrow prophesied by Simeon, save us from degeneration, disaster, and war. Protect us from all harm. O sorrowful and immaculate heart of Mary, you who bore the sufferings of your son in the depths of your heart be our advocate. Pray for us, that acting always according to your will and the will of your divine son, we may live and die pleasing to God. Amen.

Saint Juan Diego

DECEMBER 9TH OPTIONAL MEMORIAL

COLLECT PRAYER
O God, who by means of Saint Juan Diego showed the love of the most holy Virgin Mary for your people, grant, through his intercession, that, by following the counsels our Mother gave at Guadalupe, we may be ever constant in fulfilling your will. Through our Lord Jesus Christ, your Son, who lives and reigns with you in the unity of the Holy Spirit, one God, for ever and ever. Amen.

CANONIZATION OF JUAN DIEGO CUAUHTLATOATZIN

HOMILY OF THE HOLY FATHER JOHN PAUL II Mexico City, 2002

Blessed Juan Diego, a good, Christian Indian, whom simple people have always considered a saint! We ask you to accompany the Church on her pilgrimage in Mexico, so that she may be more evangelizing and more missionary each day. Encourage the Bishops, support the priests, inspire new and holy vocations, help all those who give their lives to the cause of Christ and the spread of his Kingdom.

Happy Juan Diego, true and faithful man! We entrust to you our lay brothers and sisters so that, feeling the call to holiness, they may imbue every area of social life with the spirit of the Gospel. Bless families, strengthen spouses in their marriage, sustain the efforts of parents to give their children a Christian upbringing. Look with favour upon the pain of those who are suffering in body or in spirit, on those afflicted by poverty, loneliness, marginalization or ignorance. May all people, civic leaders and ordinary citizens, always act in accordance with the demands of justice and with respect for the dignity of each person, so that in this way peace may be reinforced.

Beloved Juan Diego, "the talking eagle"! Show us the way that leads to the "Dark Virgin" of Tepeyac, that she may receive us in the depths of her heart, for she is the loving, compassionate Mother who guides us to the true God. Amen.

Our Lady of Loreto

DECEMBER 10TH HISTORICAL

COLLECT PRAYER
O God, who at the announcement of your angel willed that your Word would take flesh in the womb of the Blessed Virgin Mary, grant, we pray, to us who remember this great mystery in this holy place, the ability to celebrate both in faith and in holiness of life, the immensity of your mercy. Through our Lord Jesus Christ, your Son, who lives and reigns with you in the unity of the Holy Spirit, one God, forever and ever. Amen.

PRAYER TO OUR LADY OF LORETO

O Mary, Immaculate Virgin, for the sake of your blessed house, which we the angels moved to the pleasant hills of Loreto, turn your benevolent eyes toward us.
For the holy walls within which you were born and lived as a child, with prayers and the most sublime love; for the fortunate walls that listened to the greetings of the angel who called you: "Blessed among all women" and which remind us of the incarnation of the word in your

purest bosom; for your blessed house, where you lived with Jesus and Joseph, and which became during the centuries the fervently longed-for destination of the saints, who considered themselves lucky to kiss fervently your sacred walls, bestow upon us the graces which we humbly ask, and the fortune of coming to heaven after the exile, to repeat to you the greetings of the angel: HAIL MARY. Amen.

Litany of Loreto

The Litany of the Blessed Virgin Mary is a Marian litany originally approved in 1587 by Pope Sixtus V. Also known as the Litany of the Blessed Virgin Mary, it's been in use at the Marian shrine in Loreto, Italy since at least 1558. The litany is usually recited as a call and response in a group setting. A partial indulgence is attached to the prayer at any time. We recite The Litany of Loreto on all Marian feast days. The versicle and prayer after the litany may be varied by season. Included at the end of the prayer here is the versicle and prayer for Eastertide.

V	R
Lord, have mercy on us.	Christ, have mercy on us.
Lord, have mercy on us.	Christ, have mercy on us.
Christ, hear us.	Christ, graciously hear us.

God the Father of Heaven,	Have mercy on us.
God the Son, Redeemer of the world,	Have mercy on us.
God the Holy Spirit,	Have mercy on us.
Holy Trinity, One God,	Have mercy on us.

Holy Mary,	Pray for us.
Holy Mother of God,	Pray for us.
Holy Virgin of virgins,	Pray for us.
Mother of Christ,	Pray for us.
Mother of the Church,	Pray for us.
Mother of divine grace,	Pray for us.
Mother most pure,	Pray for us.
Mother most chaste,	Pray for us.
Mother inviolate,	Pray for us.
Mother undefiled,	Pray for us.
Mother most amiable,	Pray for us.
Mother most admirable,	Pray for us.
Mother of good counsel,	Pray for us.
Mother of our Creator,	Pray for us.
Mother of our Savior,	Pray for us.
Virgin most prudent,	Pray for us.
Virgin most venerable,	Pray for us.
Virgin most renowned,	Pray for us.
Virgin most powerful,	Pray for us.
Virgin most merciful,	Pray for us.

continued

V	R
Vessel of honor,	Pray for us.
Singular vessel of devotion,	Pray for us.
Mystical rose,	Pray for us.
Tower of David,	Pray for us.
Tower of ivory,	Pray for us.
House of gold,	Pray for us.
Ark of the covenant,	Pray for us.
Gate of Heaven,	Pray for us.
Morning star,	Pray for us.
Health of the sick,	Pray for us.
Refuge of sinners,	Pray for us.
Comforter of the afflicted,	Pray for us.
Help of Christians,	Pray for us.
Queen of angels,	Pray for us.
Queen of patriarchs,	Pray for us.
Queen of prophets,	Pray for us.
Queen of apostles,	Pray for us.
Queen of martyrs,	Pray for us.
Queen of confessors,	Pray for us.
Queen of virgins,	Pray for us.
Queen of all saints,	Pray for us.
Queen conceived without Original Sin,	Pray for us.
Queen assumed into Heaven,	Pray for us.
Queen of the holy Rosary,	Pray for us.
Queen of families,	Pray for us.
Queen of peace,	Pray for us.

Lamb of God, who takes away the sins of the world,	Spare us, O Lord.
Lamb of God, who takes away the sins of the world,	Graciously spare us, O Lord.
Lamb of God, who takes away the sins of the world,	Have mercy on us.

Pray for us, O holy Mother of God,   That we may be made worthy of the promises of Christ.

Let us pray.
Grant, we beseech thee, O Lord God, that we, your servants, may enjoy perpetual health of mind and body; and by the intercession of the Blessed Mary, ever Virgin, may be delivered from present sorrow, and obtain eternal joy. Through Christ our Lord.   Amen.

Our Lady of Guadalupe

DECEMBER 12TH FEAST

COLLECT PRAYER

O God, Father of mercies, who placed your people under the singular protection of your Son's most holy Mother, grant that all who invoke the Blessed Virgin of Guadalupe, may seek with ever more lively faith the progress of peoples in the ways of justice and of peace. Through our Lord Jesus Christ, your Son, who lives and reigns with you in the unity of the Holy Spirit, one God, for ever and ever. Amen.

NICAN MOPOHUA *A description of the Apparitions of Our Lady of Guadalupe written in Nahuatl, perhaps by Don Antonio Valeriano in the mid-16th century. The English translation is by a priest of the Oblates of Mary in the 1980s. This excerpt describes the second apparition—on Saturday, December 9.*

When he saw her, he fell at once to his knees, and bowing low before her, said: "My Little Patroness, my Lady, Queen, my smallest daughter, I went where you sent me in order to fulfill your amiable voice, amiable word. Although it was difficult for me to enter the place where the Governing Priest lives, I saw him and before him I exposed your voice, your word, as you requested. He received me kindly and listened perfectly, but from what he answered me, it seemed as if he did not understand and was not sure.

He said to me: you will come another time. I will calmly listen to you from the beginning and I will see why you came, your desire, your will. I believe, according to the way he answered me, he thinks the house you want them to build here for you may be my invention, or maybe it does not come from your lips.

I beg you very much, my Lady, Queen, my little girl, entrust one of the noblemen, someone who is esteemed, who is known, respected, honored, to direct, to carry

out your amiable wish, your amiable word, so that they will believe him. Because truly I am a man of the fields, I myself need to be led; I am like a beast of burden, like a tail, like a wing, to be loaded with a burden. It is not up to me to decide the place where I go or where I stop. Please forgive me, I will afflict your countenance, your heart with sorrow; I will fall in your anger, in your displeasure. Lady, my owner, I belong to you."

The Perfect Virgin, worthy of honor and veneration, answered him: "Listen, the smallest of my sons, be assured that those who serve me, my messengers, entrusted to carry my voice, my word, to accomplish my will, are not few in number: But it is very necessary that you personally go, request that my wish, my will, be realized, be carried out, through your intercession. I beg you earnestly, youngest son of mine, and solemnly do command you that once again tomorrow you go to see the bishop.

From my part, let him know, let him hear my wish, my will, so that he will make, he will build the temple that I ask. So, once again, tell him that it is I personally, the ever virgin, holy Mary, the Mother of God who is sending you."

Saint Lucy

DECEMBER 13TH MEMORIAL

S. LVCIA

COLLECT PRAYER
May the glorious intercession of the Virgin and Martyr Saint Lucy give us a new heart, we pray, O Lord, so that we may celebrate her heavenly birthday in this present age and so behold things eternal. Through our Lord Jesus Christ, your Son, who lives and reigns with you in the unity of the Holy Spirit, one God, for ever and ever.
Amen.

PRAYER TO SAINT LUCY OF SYACUSE

O God, our Creator and Redeemer, mercifully hear our prayers that as we venerate your servant, Saint Lucy, for the light of faith you bestowed upon her, you would increase and preserve this same light in our souls, that we may be able to avoid evil, to do good and to abhor nothing so much as the Blindness and the darkness of evil and of sin.

Relying on your goodness, O God, we humbly ask you, by the intercession of your servant, Saint Lucy that you would give perfect vision to our eyes, that they may serve for your greater honor and glory, and for the salvation of our souls in this world, that we may come to the enjoyment of the unfailing light of the Lamb of God in paradise.

Saint Lucy, virgin and martyr, hear our prayers and obtain our petitions. Amen.

This Little Light of Mine

Written for children in the early twentieth century by Harry Dixon Loes, this gospel hymn later came to be associated with the civil rights movement of the 1960s. It's also appropriate for the feast of Saint Lucy—the saint of light—and for Candlemas.

This little light of mine,
I'm gonna let it shine;
This little light of mine,
I'm gonna let it shine;
This little light of mine,
I'm gonna let it shine;
Let it shine, let it shine, let it shine.

Hide it under a bushel? No!
I'm gonna let it shine;
Hide it under a bushel? No!
I'm gonna let it shine;
Hide it under a bushel? No!
I'm gonna let it shine;
Let it shine, let it shine, let it shine.

Everywhere I go,
I'm gonna let it shine;
Everywhere I go,
I'm gonna let it shine;
Everywhere I go,
I'm gonna let it shine;
Let it shine, let it shine, let it shine.

Jesus gave it to me;
I'm gonna let it shine;
Jesus gave it to me;
I'm gonna let it shine;
Jesus gave it to me;
I'm gonna let it shine;
Let it shine, let it shine, let it shine.

Saint John of the Cross

DECEMBER 14TH MEMORIAL

COLLECT PRAYER
O God, who gave the Priest Saint John an outstanding dedication to perfect self-denial and love of the Cross, grant that, by imitating him closely at all times, we may come to contemplate eternally your glory. Through our Lord Jesus Christ, your Son, who lives and reigns with you in the unity of the Holy Spirit, one God, for ever and ever. Amen.

A SPIRITUAL CANTICLE OF THE SOUL AND THE BRIDEGROOM CHRIST

by Saint John of the Cross, excerpt, translated by Rhina P. Espaillat

I have let myself be lost and bound.
We shall weave emeralds, flowers
picked when the earliest rays of morning shine,
garlands grown by the powers
of your own love, to twine
about a single strand, a hair of mine.
One hair you chanced to note,
about my neck, that did your glance awaken.
You glimpsed it at my throat,
were snared and shaken,
and wounded by my eye and wholly taken.
Whenever you beheld me,
your eyes imprinted all their graces there,
mastered and quelled me;
and my eyes earned their share:
to worship all in you that sight laid bare.
Do not, I beg, despise
the swarthy skin in which your sight first knew me;
look on me now: your eyes
have scattered through me
the beauty of the gaze with which you drew me.
That snowy little dove
bearing the branch back to the ark is flying
the turtle, high above
happily spying
on the green banks the Love for which she's sighing.

She once lived lonely,
and now, alone, has settled in her nest,
guided alone and only
by One she loves the best,
who, wounded for love's sake, has come to rest.
Let us find joy together,
Beloved, in your beauty find our looks
reflected, whether
on hills or in pure brooks;
let us go deep into those wooded nooks.
Then to high, hidden
crevices in stony desert waste
caves none can find unbidden
we'll go, untraced,
where pomegranate wine is ours to taste.
You would delight me, showing
me, there, those things my spirit yearns to know,
and later by bestowing,
O Love I treasure so!
what first you gave to me some days ago.
Air, in its even breathing;
the song sweet Philomel sings in her flight;
the grove, its peace bequeathing
to gentle night,
with flames consuming all in painless light.
And none to apprehend it;
Aminadab quite gone, without a trace;
the siege quietly ended,
horsemen halting their race,
dismounting near the waters of that place.

Christmas Novena

NINE DAYS OF PRAYER AND SCRIPTURE TO PREPARE OUR HEARTS FOR CHRISTMAS, USUALLY USED DECEMBER 16-24

This Christmas Novena has been a part of our family's preparation for Christmas for over a decade now. We have a lot of liturgical living traditions in our home, but if I had to choose just one, I would say that this Novena has been the most meaningful of them all.

It includes beautiful prayers, Old and New Testament scripture readings, and an Advent hymn sing along with the traditional O Antiphons. It takes 15 or 20 minutes to finish, depending on the length of the readings.

This Novena is traditionally said from December 16-24. In our family, we usually start it a day early, because we often have had friends and neighbors join us, who have other obligations on Christmas Eve. And even on years when it's just been our family, it's nice to have an extra day, in case something comes up and we miss one.

Ideally, we start the prayers after dinner, with the house tidied and the kids in their jammies. We'll say the Novena prayers, then read a story from our Advent/Christmas book stack, and have a little bedtime snack.

Non-ideally, we've sometimes done it at breakfast, in the car, over Facetime, in a not tidy house, and with a toddler sitting on a potty.

However we can make it happen, these nine days of prayer together really deepen Advent for us and help us to keep our focus where it belongs in the fun, crazy, beautiful days before Christmas.

Opening prayers

Recited on each of the nine days.

LEADER 1: O Lord, open my lips.
ALL: And my mouth shall proclaim Your praise.

LEADER 1: O God, come to my assistance.
ALL: O Lord, make haste to help me. Glory to the Father and to the Son and to the Holy Spirit. As it was in the beginning, is now and will be forever. Amen. Alleluia.

LEADER 1: Our Lord and King is drawing near, O come, let us adore Him.
ALL: Our Lord and King is drawing near, O come, let us adore Him.

LEADER 2: Rejoice, O you daughter of Sion and exult fully, O daughter of Jerusalem! Behold, the Lord and Master comes, and there shall be a brilliant light in that day, and the mountains shall drop down sweetness, and hills flow with milk and honey, for in that day the Great Prophet will come, and He Himself will renew Jerusalem.
ALL: Our Lord and King is drawing near, O come, let us adore Him.

LEADER 2: Behold, the God-man of the house of David will come to sit upon the royal throne, and you will see Him and your heart will rejoice.
ALL: O come, let us adore Him.

LEADER 2: Behold, the Lord our Protector will come to save us, Israel's holy One, wearing the crown of royalty on His noble brow and He will exercise His rule from sea to shining sea, and from the waters of the river to the ends of the earth.
ALL: O come, let us adore Him.

Let the Heavens Be Glad

Recited on each of the nine days. Take turns saying the response lines.

ALL: Blow ye the trumpet in Sion, for the day of the Lord is nigh: behold, He will come to save us, alleluia, alleluia!

RESPONSE:

~Let the heavens be glad and the earth rejoice. O all you mountains, praise the Lord.

~Let the mountains break forth into gladness, and the hills with justice.

~For the Lord shall come and to the poor He shall show mercy.

~Drop down dew, you heavens, from above and let the clouds rain the Just One;

~Let the earth be opened and bud forth the Savior.

~Be mindful of us, O Lord, and visit us in Your salvation.

~Show to us, O Lord, Your mercy, and grant us your salvation.

~Come, O Lord, in peace visit us that with a perfect heart we may rejoice before You.

~Come, O Lord, do not tarry; do away with the offenses of your people.

~Come and show to us your countenance, O Lord. You sit upon the cherubim.

LEADER 1: Glory to the Father and the Son and to the Holy Spirit.
ALL: As it was in the beginning, is now and will be forever. Amen.

ALL: Blow ye the trumpet in Sion, for the day of the Lord is nigh: behold, He will come to save us, alleluia, alleluia!

LEADER 2: Behold, the Lord and King will appear, and he will not deceive; but if he should delay, wait for him to come; he will surely come and will not tarry.
ALL: O come, let us adore him.

LEADER 2: The Lord will come down like rain upon the fleece of Gideon; justice will thrive and an abundance of true peace; all the kings of the lands of the earth will adore him, and every nation will serve him.
ALL: O come, let us adore him.

LEADER 2: A Child will be born to us, and he will be called God the almighty; he will sit upon the royal throne of David his father, and he will hold sway, the sign of his power on his shoulder.
ALL: O come, let us adore him.

LEADER 2: Bethlehem, city of the Most High God, from you will come forth the King of Israel, and he will proceed forth from his eternity; and he will be greatly praised in the midst of the entire universe; and there will be peace in our land when he will have come.
ALL: Our Lord and King is drawing near, O come, let us adore him.

On the last day of the Novena, add:

LEADER 2: Tomorrow the wickedness of the whole world will be destroyed, and over us will reign the Savior of the world.
ALL: Our Lord and King is drawing near, O come, let us adore him.

LEADER 2: Near at last is Christ our King.
ALL: O come, let us adore him.

Readings day 1   December 16

GENESIS 3:1-15

A reading from the book of Genesis.

Now the snake was the most cunning of all the wild animals that the Lord God had made.

He asked the woman, "Did God really say, 'You shall not eat from any of the trees in the garden'?"

The woman answered the snake: "We may eat of the fruit of the trees in the garden; it is only about the fruit of the tree in the middle of the garden that God said, 'You shall not eat it or even touch it, or else you will die.'"

But the snake said to the woman: "You certainly will not die! God knows well that when you eat of it your eyes will be opened and you will be like gods, who know good and evil."

The woman saw that the tree was good for food and pleasing to the eyes, and the tree was desirable for gaining wisdom.

So she took some of its fruit and ate it; and she also gave some to her husband, who was with her, and he ate it.

Then the eyes of both of them were opened, and they knew that they were naked; so they sewed fig leaves together and made loincloths for themselves.

When they heard the sound of the Lord God walking about in the garden at the breezy time of the day, the man and his wife hid themselves from the Lord God among the trees of the garden.

The Lord God then called to the man and asked him: Where are you?

He answered, "I heard you in the garden; but I was afraid, because I was naked, so I hid."

Then God asked: Who told you that you were naked?

Have you eaten from the tree of which I had forbidden you to eat?

The man replied, "The woman whom you put here with me—she gave me fruit from the tree, so I ate it."

The Lord God then asked the woman: What is this you have done?

The woman answered, "The snake tricked me, so I ate it."

Then the Lord God said to the snake:

Because you have done this, cursed are you among all the animals, tame or wild; On your belly you shall crawl, and dust you shall eat all the days of your life.

I will put enmity between you and the woman, and between your offspring and hers; They will strike at your head, while you strike at their heel.

The word of the Lord.

ALL: Thanks be to God.

ROMANS 1:15-25

December 16

A reading from the letter of Saint Paul to the Romans.

I am eager to preach the gospel also to you in Rome.

For I am not ashamed of the gospel. It is the power of God for the salvation of everyone who believes: for Jew first, and then Greek.

For in it is revealed the righteousness of God from faith to faith; as it is written, "The one who is righteous by faith will live."

The wrath of God is indeed being revealed from heaven against every impiety and wickedness of those who suppress the truth by their wickedness.

For what can be known about God is evident to them, because God made it evident to them. Ever since the creation of the world, his invisible attributes of eternal power and divinity have been able to be understood and perceived in what he has made.

As a result, they have no excuse; for although they knew God they did not accord him glory as God or give him thanks. Instead, they became vain in their reasoning, and their senseless minds were darkened.

While claiming to be wise, they became fools and exchanged the glory of the immortal God for the likeness of an image of mortal man or of birds or of four-legged animals or of snakes.

Therefore, God handed them over to impurity through the lusts of their hearts for the mutual degradation of their bodies. They exchanged the truth of God for a lie and revered and worshiped the creature rather than the creator, who is blessed forever. Amen.

The word of the Lord.

ALL: Thanks be to God.

Readings day 2 December 17

GENESIS 3:14-20

A reading from the book of Genesis.

Then the Lord God said to the
  snake:
Because you have done this,
  cursed are you among all the
  animals, tame or wild;
On your belly you shall crawl,
  and dust you shall eat
  all the days of your life.
I will put enmity between you and
  the woman, and between your
offspring and hers;
They will strike at your head,
  while you strike at their heel.
To the woman he said:
I will intensify your toil in childbearing;
  in pain you shall bring forth children.
Yet your urge shall be for your husband,
  and he shall rule over you.
To the man he said: Because you listened to your wife
and ate from the tree about which I commanded you,
You shall not eat from it,
Cursed is the ground because of you!
  In toil you shall eat its yield all the days of your life.
Thorns and thistles it shall bear for you,
  and you shall eat the grass of the field.
By the sweat of your brow
  you shall eat bread,
Until you return to the ground,
  from which you were taken;
For you are dust,
  and to dust you shall return.
The man gave his wife the name "Eve," because she was
the mother of all the living.

The word of the Lord.

ALL: Thanks be to God.

ROMANS 5:12-21

December 17

A reading from the letter of Saint Paul to the Romans.

Therefore, just as through one person sin entered the world, and through sin, death, and thus death came to all, inasmuch as all sinned for up to the time of the law, sin was in the world, though sin is not accounted when there is no law. But death reigned from Adam to Moses, even over those who did not sin after the pattern of the trespass of Adam, who is the type of the one who was to come.

But the gift is not like the transgression. For if by that one person's transgression the many died, how much more did the grace of God and the gracious gift of the one person Jesus Christ overflow for the many.

And the gift is not like the result of the one person's sinning. For after one sin there was the judgment that brought condemnation; but the gift, after many transgressions, brought acquittal.

For if, by the transgression of one person, death came to reign through that one, how much more will those who receive the abundance of grace and of the gift of justification come to reign in life through the one person Jesus Christ.

In conclusion, just as through one transgression condemnation came upon all, so through one righteous act acquittal and life came to all. For just as through the disobedience of one person the many were made sinners, so through the obedience of one the many will be made righteous. The law entered in so that transgression might increase but, where sin increased, grace overflowed all the more, so that, as sin reigned in death, grace also might reign through justification for eternal life through Jesus Christ our Lord.

The word of the Lord.

ALL: Thanks be to God.

Readings day 3
December 18

GENESIS 17:15-22

A reading from the book of Genesis.

God further said to Abraham: As for Sarai your wife, do not call her Sarai; her name will be Sarah. I will bless her, and I will give you a son by her. Her also will I bless; she will give rise to nations, and rulers of peoples will issue from her.

Abraham fell face down and laughed as he said to himself, "Can a child be born to a man who is a hundred years old? Can Sarah give birth at ninety?" So Abraham said to God, "If only Ishmael could live in your favor!"

God replied: Even so, your wife Sarah is to bear you a son, and you shall call him Isaac. It is with him that I will maintain my covenant as an everlasting covenant and with his descendants after him.

Now as for Ishmael, I will heed you: I hereby bless him. I will make him fertile and will multiply him exceedingly. He will become the father of twelve chieftains, and I will make of him a great nation. But my covenant I will maintain with Isaac, whom Sarah shall bear to you by this time next year.

When he had finished speaking with Abraham, God departed from him.

The word of the Lord.

ALL: Thanks be to God.

ROMANS 4:13-23

December 18

A reading from the letter of Saint Paul to the Romans.

It was not through the law that the promise was made to Abraham and his descendants that he would inherit the world, but through the righteousness that comes from faith.

For if those who adhere to the law are the heirs, faith is null and the promise is void. For the law produces wrath; but where there is no law, neither is there violation.

For this reason, it depends on faith, so that it may be a gift, and the promise may be guaranteed to all his descendants, not to those who only adhere to the law but to those who follow the faith of Abraham, who is the father of all of us, as it is written, "I have made you father of many nations." He is our father in the sight of God, in whom he believed, who gives life to the dead and calls into being what does not exist.

He believed, hoping against hope, that he would become "the father of many nations," according to what was said, "Thus shall your descendants be." He did not weaken in faith when he considered his own body as already dead (for he was almost a hundred years old) and the dead womb of Sarah.

He did not doubt God's promise in unbelief; rather, he was empowered by faith and gave glory to God and was fully convinced that what he had promised he was also able to do.

That is why "it was credited to him as righteousness." But it was not for him alone that it was written that "it was credited to him."

The word of the Lord.

ALL: Thanks be to God.

Readings day 4 — December 19

DEUTERONOMY 15:12-20

A reading from the book of Deuteronomy.

If your kin, a Hebrew man or woman, sells himself or herself to you, he or she is to serve you for six years, but in the seventh year you shall release him or her as a free person. When you release a male from your service, as a free person, you shall not send him away empty-handed, but shall weigh him down with gifts from your flock and threshing floor and wine press; as the Lord, your God, has blessed you, so you shall give to him.

For remember that you too were slaves in the land of Egypt, and the Lord, your God, redeemed you. That is why I am giving you this command today. But if he says to you, "I do not wish to leave you," because he loves you and your household, since he is well off with you, you shall take an awl and put it through his ear into the door, and he shall be your slave forever.

Your female slave, also, you shall treat in the same way. Do not be reluctant when you let them go free, since the service they have given you for six years was worth twice a hired laborer's salary; and the Lord, your God, will bless you in everything you do.

You shall consecrate to the Lord, your God, every male firstling born in your herd and in your flock. You shall not work the firstlings of your cattle, nor shear the firstlings of your flock. In the presence of the Lord, your God, you shall eat them year after year, you and your household, in the place that the Lord will choose.

The word of the Lord.

ALL: Thanks be to God.

December 19

ACTS 3:18-26

A reading from the Acts of the Apostles.

But God has thus brought to fulfillment what he had announced beforehand through the mouth of all the prophets, that his Messiah would suffer.

Repent, therefore, and be converted, that your sins may be wiped away, and that the Lord may grant you times of refreshment and send you the Messiah already appointed for you,

Jesus, whom heaven must receive until the times of universal restoration of which God spoke through the mouth of his holy prophets from of old.

For Moses said:

'A prophet like me will the Lord, your God, raise up for
 you from among your own kinsmen;
to him you shall listen in all that he may say to you.
Everyone who does not listen to that prophet
 will be cut off from the people.'

Moreover, all the prophets who spoke, from Samuel and those afterwards, also announced these days.

You are the children of the prophets and of the covenant that God made with your ancestors when he said to Abraham, 'In your offspring all the families of the earth shall be blessed.'

For you first, God raised up his servant and sent him to bless you by turning each of you from your evil ways."

The word of the Lord.

ALL: Thanks be to God.

Readings day 5 — December 20

ISAIAH 28:14-20

A reading from the Prophet Isaiah.

Therefore, hear the word of the Lord, you scoffers,
 who rule this people in Jerusalem:
You have declared, "We have made a covenant with
 death, with Sheol we have made a pact;
When the raging flood passes through,
 it will not reach us;
For we have made lies our refuge,
 and in falsehood we have found a hiding place,"—

Therefore, thus says the Lord God:
 See, I am laying a stone in Zion,
 a stone that has been tested,
A precious cornerstone as a sure foundation;
 whoever puts faith in it will not waver.
I will make judgment a measuring line,
 and justice a level.—
Hail shall sweep away the refuge of lies,
 and waters shall flood the hiding place.
Your covenant with death shall be canceled
 and your pact with Sheol shall not stand.
When the raging flood passes through,
 you shall be beaten down by it.
Whenever it passes, it shall seize you;
 morning after morning
 it shall pass,
 by day and
 by night.
Sheer terror
 to impart
 the message!
For the bed shall be too short to stretch
 out in, and the cover too narrow to wrap in.

The word of the Lord.

ALL: Thanks be to God.

December 20

THOU ARE THE KING OF GLORY O CHRIST

ROMANS 10:5-11

A reading from the letter of Saint Paul to the Romans.

Moses writes about the righteousness that comes from the law, "The one who does these things will live by them." But the righteousness that comes from faith says, "Do not say in your heart, 'Who will go up into heaven?' (that is, to bring Christ down) or 'Who will go down into the abyss?' (that is, to bring Christ up from the dead)." But what does it say?

"The word is near you,
   in your mouth and
   in your heart"

(that is, the word of faith that we preach), for, if you confess with your mouth that Jesus is Lord and believe in your heart that God raised him from the dead, you will be saved. For one believes with the heart and so is justified, and one confesses with the mouth and so is saved. For the scripture says, "No one who believes in him will be put to shame."

The word of the Lord.

ALL: Thanks be to God.

Readings day 6
December 21

1 SAMUEL 2:1-10

A reading from the first book of Samuel.

"My heart exults in the Lord,
   my horn is exalted by my God.
I have swallowed up my enemies;
   I rejoice in your victory.
There is no Holy One like the Lord;
   there is no Rock like our God.
Speak boastfully no longer,
   Do not let arrogance issue from your mouths.
For an all-knowing God is the Lord,
   a God who weighs actions.
"The bows of the mighty are broken,
   while the tottering gird on strength.
The well-fed hire themselves out for bread,
   while the hungry no longer have to toil.
The barren wife bears seven sons,
   while the mother of many languishes.
"The Lord puts to death and gives life,
   casts down to Sheol and brings up again.
The Lord makes poor and makes rich,
   humbles, and also exalts.
He raises the needy from the dust;
   from the ash heap lifts up the poor,
To seat them with nobles
   and make a glorious throne their heritage.
"For the pillars of the earth are the Lord's,
   and he has set the world upon them.
He guards the footsteps of his faithful ones,
   but the wicked shall perish in the darkness;
   for not by strength does one prevail.
The Lord's foes shall be shattered;
   the Most High in heaven thunders;
   the Lord judges the ends of the earth.
May he give strength to his king,
   and exalt the horn of his anointed!"

The word of the Lord.

ALL: Thanks be to God.

December 21

LUKE 1:26-39

A reading from the Holy Gospel according to Saint Luke.

In the sixth month, the angel Gabriel was sent from God to a town of Galilee called Nazareth, to a virgin betrothed to a man named Joseph, of the house of David, and the virgin's name was Mary.

And coming to her, he said, "Hail, favored one! The Lord is with you."

But she was greatly troubled at what was said and pondered what sort of greeting this might be.

Then the angel said to her, "Do not be afraid, Mary, for you have found favor with God.

Behold, you will conceive in your womb and bear a son, and you shall name him Jesus.

He will be great and will be called Son of the Most High, and the Lord God will give him the throne of David his father, and he will rule over the house of Jacob forever, and of his kingdom there will be no end."

But Mary said to the angel, "How can this be, since I have no relations with a man?"

And the angel said to her in reply, "The holy Spirit will come upon you, and the power of the Most High will overshadow you.

Therefore the child to be born will be called holy, the Son of God.

And behold, Elizabeth, your relative, has also conceived a son in her old age, and this is the sixth month for her who was called barren; for nothing will be impossible for God."

December 21

Mary said, "Behold, I am the handmaid of the Lord. May it be done to me according to your word."

Then the angel departed from her.

During those days Mary set out and traveled to the hill country in haste to a town of Judah.

The Gospel of the Lord.

ALL: Praise to you, Lord Jesus Christ.

Readings day 7
December 22

DEUTERONOMY 7:6-21

A reading from the book of Deuteronomy.

For you are a people holy to the Lord, your God; the Lord, your God, has chosen you from all the peoples on the face of the earth to be a people specially his own.

It was not because you are more numerous than all the peoples that the Lord set his heart on you and chose you; for you are really the smallest of all peoples. It was because the Lord loved you and because of his fidelity to the oath he had sworn to your ancestors, that the Lord brought you out with a strong hand and redeemed you from the house of slavery, from the hand of Pharaoh, king of Egypt.

Know, then, that the Lord, your God, is God: the faithful God who keeps covenant mercy to the thousandth generation toward those who love him and keep his commandments, but who repays with destruction those who hate him; he does not delay with those who hate him, but makes them pay for it.

Therefore carefully observe the commandment, the statutes and the ordinances which I command you today.

As your reward for heeding these ordinances and keeping them carefully, the Lord, your God, will keep with you the covenant mercy he promised on oath to your ancestors.

He will love and bless and multiply you; he will bless the fruit of your womb and the produce of your soil, your grain and wine and oil, the young of your herds and the offspring of your flocks, in the land which he swore to your ancestors he would give you. You will be blessed above all peoples; no man or woman among you shall be childless nor shall your livestock be barren.

DEUTERONOMY 7:15-21

December 22

The Lord will remove all sickness from you; he will not afflict you with any of the malignant diseases that you know from Egypt, but will leave them with all those who hate you.

You shall consume all the peoples which the Lord, your God, is giving over to you. You are not to look on them with pity, nor serve their gods, for that would be a snare to you. If you say to yourselves, "These nations are more numerous than we. How can we dispossess them?" do not be afraid of them. Rather, remember clearly what the Lord, your God, did to Pharaoh and to all Egypt: the great testings which your own eyes have seen, the signs and wonders, the strong hand and outstretched arm with which the Lord, your God, brought you out. The same also will he do to all the peoples of whom you are now afraid.

Moreover, the Lord, your God, will send hornets among them, until those who are left and those who are hiding from you are destroyed. Therefore, do not be terrified by them, for the Lord, your God, who is in your midst, is a great and awesome God.

The word of the Lord.

ALL: Thanks be to God.

Readings day 8 December 23

ISAIAH 7:10-16

A reading from the Prophet Isaiah.

Again the Lord spoke to Ahaz:

Ask for a sign from the Lord, your God; let it be deep as Sheol, or high as the sky!

But Ahaz answered, "I will not ask! I will not tempt the Lord!"

Then he said: Listen, house of David! Is it not enough that you weary human beings? Must you also weary my God?

Therefore the Lord himself will give you a sign; the young woman, pregnant and about to bear a son, shall name him Emmanuel.

Curds and honey he will eat so that he may learn to reject evil and choose good; for before the child learns to reject evil and choose good, the land of those two kings whom you dread shall be deserted.

The word of the Lord.

ALL: Thanks be to God.

December 23

MATTHEW 1:18-25

A reading from the Holy Gospel according to Saint Matthew.

Now this is how the birth of Jesus Christ came about. When his mother Mary was betrothed to Joseph, but before they lived together, she was found with child through the holy Spirit. Joseph her husband, since he was a righteous man, yet unwilling to expose her to shame, decided to divorce her quietly. Such was his intention when, behold, the angel of the Lord appeared to him in a dream and said, "Joseph, son of David, do not be afraid to take Mary your wife into your home. For it is through the holy Spirit that this child has been conceived in her. She will bear a son and you are to name him Jesus, because he will save his people from their sins." All this took place to fulfill what the Lord had said through the prophet:

"Behold, the virgin shall be with child and bear a son, and they shall name him Emmanuel,"

which means "God is with us." When Joseph awoke, he did as the angel of the Lord had commanded him and took his wife into his home. He had no relations with her until she bore a son, and he named him Jesus.

The Gospel of the Lord.

ALL: Praise to you, Lord Jesus Christ.

Readings day 9 — December 24

MICAH 5:1-5

A reading from the Prophet Micah.

But you, Bethlehem-
Ephrathah
least among
the clans of
Judah,
From you shall
come forth for me one who is to be ruler in Israel;
Whose origin is from of old,
from ancient times.
Therefore the Lord will give them up, until the time
when she who is to give birth has borne,
Then the rest of his kindred shall return
to the children of Israel.
He shall take his place as shepherd
by the strength of the Lord,
by the majestic name of the Lord, his God;

And they shall dwell securely, for now
his greatness
shall reach to the ends of the earth:
he shall be peace.
If Assyria invades our country
and treads upon our land,
We shall raise against it seven shepherds,
eight of royal standing;
They shall tend the land of Assyria
with the sword,
and the land of Nimrod with the drawn sword;
They will deliver us from Assyria,
when it invades our land,
when it treads upon our borders.

The word of the Lord.

ALL: Thanks be to God.

December 24

LUKE 2:1-7

A reading from the Holy Gospel according to Saint Luke.

In those days a decree went out from Caesar Augustus that the whole world should be enrolled. This was the first enrollment, when Quirinius was governor of Syria.

So all went to be enrolled, each to his own town.

And Joseph too went up from Galilee from the town of Nazareth to Judea, to the city of David that is called Bethlehem, because he was of the house and family of David, to be enrolled with Mary, his betrothed, who was with child.

While they were there, the time came for her to have her child, and she gave birth to her firstborn son.

She wrapped him in swaddling clothes and laid him in a manger, because there was no room for them in the inn.

The Gospel of the Lord.

ALL: Praise to you, Lord Jesus Christ.

After the readings:

LEADER 1: Drop down dew from above, O you heavens, and let the clouds rain the just one.

The O Antiphons beg God with mounting impatience to come and save his people. The order of the antiphons climb climactically through our history of redemption. From O Sapentia, at the beginning of eternity, to O Adonai at the time of Moses, about 1100 BC, to O Radix Jesse, O Clavis David, and O Rex Gentium focused on Jesse and his son King David around 1000 BC, and finally, O Emmanuel, on the first Christmas Eve.

O Antiphons

December 16

ALL SING:

O Come, O come, Emmanuel,
And ransom captive Israel,
That mourns in lonely exile here
Until the Son of God appear.

Rejoice! Rejoice! Emmanuel
Shall come to thee,
O Israel!

Veni veni, Emmanuel
Captivum solve Israel,
Qui gemit in exsilio,
Privatus Dei Filio.

Gaude! Gaude! Emmanuel,
Nascetur pro te Israel!

O Antiphons

December 17

O SAPIENTIA :: O WISDOM

ALL SING:

O come, thou Wisdom, from on high,
And order all things far and nigh;
To us the path of knowledge show,
And teach us in her ways to go.

Rejoice! Rejoice! Emmanuel
Shall come to thee, O Israel!

Veni, O Sapientia,
Quae hic disponis omnia,
Veni, viam prudentiae
Ut doceas et gloriae.

Gaude! Gaude! Emmanuel,
Nascetur pro te Israel!

O Antiphons

December 18

O ADONAI :: O LORD

ALL SING:

O come, o come, thou Lord of might,
Who to thy tribes on Sinai's height
In ancient times did give the law,
In cloud, and majesty, and awe.

Rejoice! Rejoice! Emmanuel
Shall come to thee, O Israel!

Veni, veni, Adonai,
Qui populo in Sinai
Legem dedisti vertice
In maiestate gloriae.

Gaude! Gaude! Emmanuel,
Nascetur pro te Israel!

O Antiphons

December 19

O RADIX JESSE :: O ROOT OF JESSE

ALL SING:

O come, thou Rod of Jesse's stem,
From ev'ry foe deliver them
That trust thy mighty power to save,
And give them vict'ry o'er the grave.

Rejoice! Rejoice! Emmanuel
Shall come to thee, O Israel!

Veni, O Iesse virgula,
Ex hostis tuos ungula,
De spectu tuos tartari
Educ et antro barathri.

Gaude! Gaude! Emmanuel,
Nascetur pro te Israel!

O Antiphons
December 20

O CLAVIS DAVID :: O KEY OF DAVID

ALL SING:

O come, Thou Key of David, come,
And open wide our heav'nly home,
Make safe the way that leads on high,
That we no more have cause to sigh.

Rejoice! Rejoice! Emmanuel
Shall come to thee, O Israel!

Veni, Clavis Davidica,
Regna reclude caelica,
Fac iter tutum superum,
Et claude vias inferum.

Gaude! Gaude! Emmanuel,
Nascetur pro te Israel!

O Antiphons

O DAYSPRING
December 21

O ORIENS :: O DAYSPRING

ALL SING:

O come, Thou Dayspring from on high,
And cheer us by thy drawing nigh;
Disperse the gloomy clouds of night
And death's dark shadow put to flight.

Rejoice! Rejoice! Emmanuel
Shall come to thee, O Israel!

Veni, veni O Oriens,
Solare nos adveniens,
Noctis depelle nebulas,
Dirasque mortis tenebras.

Gaude! Gaude! Emmanuel,
Nascetur pro te Israel!

O Antiphons

O King
December 22

O REX GENTIUM :: O KING OF NATIONS

ALL SING:

O come, Desire of nations, bind
In one the hearts of all mankind;
Bid every strife and quarrel cease
And fill the world with heaven's peace.

Rejoice! Rejoice! Emmanuel
Shall come to thee, O Israel!

Veni, veni, Rex Gentium,
Veni, Redemptor omnium,
Ut salvas tuos famulos
Peccati sibi conscios.

Gaude! Gaude! Emmanuel,
Nascetur pro te Israel!

O Antiphons

December 23
O EMMANUEL :: O GOD WITH US

ALL SING:

O Come, O come, Emmanuel,
And ransom captive Israel,
That mourns in lonely exile here
Until the Son of God appear.

Rejoice! Rejoice! Emmanuel
Shall come to thee, O Israel!

Veni veni, Emmanuel
Captivum solve Israel,
Qui gemit in exsilio,
Privatus Dei Filio.

Gaude! Gaude! Emmanuel,
Nascetur pro te Israel!

O Antiphons

December 24

ALL SING:

O Come, O come, Emmanuel,
And ransom captive Israel,
That mourns in lonely exile here
Until the Son of God appear.

Rejoice! Rejoice! Emmanuel
Shall come to thee, O Israel!

Veni veni, Emmanuel
Captivum solve Israel,
Qui gemit in exsilio,
Privatus Dei Filio.

Gaude! Gaude! Emmanuel,
Nascetur pro te Israel!

Magnificat

Recited on each of the nine days.

My soul proclaims the greatness of the Lord, my spirit rejoices in God my Savior; for he has looked with favor on his lowly servant.

From this day all generations will call me blessed; the Almighty has done great things for me, and holy is his name.

He has mercy on those who fear him in every generation.

He has shown the strength of his arm, he has scattered the proud in their conceit.

He has cast down the mighty from their thrones, and has lifted up the lowly.

He has filled the hungry with good things, snd the rich He has sent away empty.

He comes to the help of his servant Israel; for he has remembered his promise of mercy, the promise he made to our fathers, to Abraham and his children for ever.

Glory to the Father and the Son and the Holy Spirit;

As it was in the beginning, is now and will be forever. Amen.

Sing the Antiphon for the day again.

Closing prayers

Recited on each of the nine days.

LEADER 1: O Lord, hear my prayer.
ALL: And let my cry come to you.

LEADER 1: Let us pray: Hasten, we beseech you, O Lord; do not delay; grant us the help of supernatural virtue, so that your coming will be a consolation to those who hope in your mercy. You who live and reign with God the Father in the unity of the Holy Spirit, God world without end.
ALL: Amen.

LEADER 1: Let us bless the Lord.
ALL: And give him thanks.

LEADER 1: May the souls of the faithful departed through the mercy of God rest in peace.
ALL: Amen.

Gaudete Sunday / Bambinelli Sunday

THIRD SUNDAY OF ADVENT SOLEMNITY/HOLYDAY OF OBLIGATION

COLLECT PRAYER
O God, who see how your people faithfully await the feast of the Lord's Nativity, enable us, we pray, to attain the joys of so great a salvation and to celebrate them always with solemn worship and glad rejoicing. Through our Lord Jesus Christ, your Son, who lives and reigns with you in the unity of the Holy Spirit, one God, for ever and ever. Amen.

ENTRANCE ANTIPHON Philippians 4:4-5
Rejoice in the Lord always; again I say, rejoice. Indeed, the Lord is near.

Gaudete in Domino semper: iterum dico, gaudete: modestia vestra nota sit omnibus hominibus: Dominus prope est.

BLESSING OF A MANGER OR NATIVITY SCENE

The blessing is given by a priest of deacon if present, but this rite is also appropriate for use when the blessing takes place in the home and is given by a family member.

All make the sign of the cross.
LEADER: Our help is in the name of the Lord.
ALL: Who made heaven and earth.

BIBLE READING *Luke 2:1-8*
A reading from the holy gospel according to Luke:
In those days a decree went out from Caesar Augustus that the whole world should be enrolled. This was the first enrollment, when Quirinius was governor of Syria. So all went to be enrolled, each to his own town. And Joseph too went up from Galilee from the town of Nazareth to Judea, to the city of David that is called Bethlehem, because he was of the house and family of David, to be enrolled with Mary, his betrothed, who was with child. While they were there, the time came for her to have her child, and she gave birth to her firstborn son. She wrapped him in swaddling clothes and laid him in a manger, because there was no room for them in the inn.

Now there were shepherds in that region living in the fields and keeping the night watch over their flock.

If the leader is a priest or deacon, he says the prayer of blessing with hands outstretched; a lay leader says the prayer with hands joined.
LEADER: God of every nation and people, from the very beginning of creation you have made manifest your love: when our need for a Savior was great you sent your Son to be born of the Virgin Mary. To our lives he brings joy and peace, justice, mercy, and love.
Lord, bless all who look upon this manger; may it remind us of the humble birth of Jesus, and raise up our thoughts to him, who is God-with-us and Savior of all, and who lives and reigns for ever and ever.
ALL: Amen.

The manger may be sprinkled with holy water.
All make the sign of the cross.

Christmas Eve / Saints Adam & Eve

DECEMBER 24 HISTORIC

COLLECT PRAYER
Pour forth, we beseech you, O Lord, your grace into our hearts, that we, to whom the Incarnation of Christ your Son was made known by the message of an Angel, may by his Passion and Cross be brought to the glory of his Resurrection. Who lives and reigns with you in the unity of the Holy Spirit, one God, for ever and ever. Amen.

THE NEW EVE *from Against Heresies, written in 180AD by St. Irenaeus*
The Lord, coming into his own creation in visible form, was sustained by his own creation which he himself sustains in being. His obedience on the tree of the cross reversed the disobedience at the tree in Eden; the good news of the truth announced by an angel to Mary, a virgin subject to a husband, undid the evil lie that seduced Eve, a virgin espoused to a husband.

As Eve was seduced by the word of an angel and so fled from God after disobeying his word, Mary in her turn was given the good news by the word of an angel, and bore God in obedience to his word. As Eve was seduced into disobedience to God, so Mary was persuaded into obedience to God; thus the Virgin Mary became the advocate of the virgin Eve.

BIBLE READING FOR THE FEAST *Genesis 2:4-3:24*

This is the story of the heavens and the earth at their creation. When the Lord God made the earth and the heavens—there was no field shrub on earth and no grass of the field had sprouted, for the Lord God had sent no rain upon the earth and there was no man to till the ground, but a stream was welling up out of the earth and watering all the surface of the ground—then the Lord God formed the man out of the dust of the ground and blew into his nostrils the breath of life, and the man became a living being.

The Lord God planted a garden in Eden, in the east, and placed there the man whom he had formed. Out of the ground the Lord God made grow every tree that was delightful to look at and good for food, with the tree of life in the middle of the garden and the tree of the knowledge of good and evil.

A river rises in Eden to water the garden; beyond there it divides and becomes four branches. The name of the first is the Pishon; it is the one that winds through the whole land of Havilah, where there is gold. The gold of that land is good; bdellium and lapis lazuli are also there. The name of the second river is the Gihon; it is the one that winds all through the land of Cush. The name of the third river is the Tigris; it is the one that flows east of Asshur. The fourth river is the Euphrates.

The Lord God then took the man and settled him in the garden of Eden, to cultivate and care for it. The Lord God gave the man this order: You are free to eat from any of the trees of the garden except the tree of knowledge of good and evil. From that tree you shall not eat; when you eat from it you shall die.

The Lord God said: It is not good for the man to be alone. I will make a helper suited to him. So the Lord God formed out of the ground all the wild animals and all the birds of the air, and he brought them to the man to see what he would call them; whatever the man called each living creature was then its name. The man gave names to all the tame animals, all the birds of the air, and all the wild animals; but none proved to be a helper suited to the man.

So the Lord God cast a deep sleep on the man, and while he was asleep, he took out one of his ribs and closed up its place with flesh. The Lord God then built the rib that he had taken from the man into a woman. When he brought her to the man, the man said:
"This one, at last, is bone of my bones
   and flesh of my flesh;
This one shall be called 'woman,'
   for out of man this one has been taken."

That is why a man leaves his father and mother and clings to his wife, and the two of them become one body.

The man and his wife were both naked, yet they felt no shame.

Now the snake was the most cunning of all the wild animals that the Lord God had made. He asked the woman, "Did God really say, 'You shall not eat from any of the trees in the garden'?" The woman answered the snake: "We may eat of the fruit of the trees in the garden; it is only about the fruit of the tree in the middle of the garden that God said, 'You shall not eat it or even touch it, or else you will die.'" But the snake said to the woman: "You certainly will not die! God knows well that when you eat of it your eyes will be opened and you will be like gods, who know good and evil." The woman saw that the tree was good for food and pleasing to the eyes, and the tree was desirable for gaining wisdom. So she took some of its fruit and ate it; and she also gave some to her husband, who was with her, and he ate it. Then the eyes of both of them were opened, and they knew that they were naked; so they sewed fig leaves together and made loincloths for themselves.

When they heard the sound of the Lord God walking about in the garden at the breezy time of the day, the man and his wife hid themselves from the Lord God among the trees of the garden. The Lord God then called to the man and asked him: Where are you? He answered, "I heard you in the garden; but I was afraid, because I was naked, so I hid." Then God asked: Who told you that you were naked? Have you eaten from the tree of which I had forbidden you to eat? The man replied, "The woman whom you put here with me—she gave me fruit from the tree, so I ate it." The Lord God then asked the woman: What is this you have done? The woman answered, "The snake tricked me, so I ate it."

Then the Lord God said to the snake:
Because you have done this,
   cursed are you
   among all the animals, tame or wild;
On your belly you shall crawl,
   and dust you shall eat
   all the days of your life.
I will put enmity between you and the woman,
   and between your offspring and hers;
They will strike at your head,
   while you strike at their heel.
To the woman he said:
I will intensify your toil in childbearing;
   in pain you shall bring forth children.
Yet your urge shall be for your husband,
   and he shall rule over you.
To the man he said: Because you listened to your wife
   and ate from the tree about which I commanded you,
You shall not eat from it,
Cursed is the ground because of you!
   In toil you shall eat its yield
   all the days of your life.
Thorns and thistles it shall bear for you,
   and you shall eat the grass of the field.
By the sweat of your brow
   you shall eat bread,
Until you return to the ground,
   from which you were taken;
For you are dust,
   and to dust you shall return.

The man gave his wife the name "Eve," because she was the mother of all the living. The Lord God made for the man and his wife garments of skin, with which he clothed them. Then the Lord God said: See! The man has become like one of us, knowing good and evil! Now, what if he also reaches out his hand to take fruit from the tree of life, and eats of it and lives forever? The Lord God therefore banished him from the garden of Eden, to till the ground from which he had been taken. He expelled the man, stationing the cherubim and the fiery revolving sword east of the garden of Eden, to guard the way to the tree of life.

Blessing & Lighting of a Christmas Tree

LEADER. Our help is in the name of the Lord.
ALL. Who has made heaven and earth.

ANTIPHON *all:* Let all the trees of the forest rejoice before the Lord who comes, who comes to govern the earth.

PSALM 96 *take turns reading stanzas:*
1. Sing to the Lord a new song;
   sing to the Lord, all the earth.
Sing to the Lord, bless his name;
   proclaim his salvation day after day.
Tell his glory among the nations;
   among all peoples, his marvelous deeds.

2. For great is the Lord and highly to be praised,
   to be feared above all gods.
For the gods of the nations are idols,
   but the Lord made the heavens.
Splendor and power go before him;
   power and grandeur are in his holy place.

3. Give to the Lord, you families of nations,
   give to the Lord glory and might;
   give to the Lord the glory due his name!
Bring gifts and enter his courts;
   bow down to the Lord, splendid in holiness.
Tremble before him, all the earth;
   declare among the nations: The Lord is king.
The world will surely stand fast, never to be shaken.
   He rules the peoples with fairness.

4. Let the heavens be glad and the earth rejoice;
   let the sea and what fills it resound;
   let the plains be joyful and all that is in them.
Then let all the trees of the forest rejoice
   before the Lord who comes,
   who comes to govern the earth,
To govern the world with justice
   and the peoples with faithfulness.

ANTIPHON REPEATED *all:* Let all the trees of the forest rejoice before the Lord who comes, who comes to govern the earth.

LEADER: A shoot shall sprout from the stump of Jesse.
ALL: And from his roots a bud shall blossom.
LEADER: The spirit of the Lord shall rest upon him.

LEADER. Lord hear my prayer.
ALL. And let my cry come to you.
LEADER. The Lord be with you.
ALL. And with your spirit.

LEADER: Let us pray.
Holy Lord, Father Almighty, Eternal God, who has caused your Son, Our Lord Jesus Christ, to be planted like a tree of life in your Church, by being born of the most Holy Virgin Mary, bless, we beseech you, this tree, that all who see it may be filled with a holy desire to be grafted as living branches onto the same Our Lord Jesus Christ, who lives and reigns with you, in the unity of the Holy Spirit, God, world without end.
ALL. Amen.

The tree is sprinkled with holy water, then lighted. End with a song.

PRAYER BEFORE BABY JESUS IN THE MANGER

The last thing we do before we go to bed on Christmas Eve, is to place the baby Jesus in the manger of our nativity scene, say this prayer, and sing Away in a Manger and Silent Night.

O Divine Redeemer Jesus Christ, prostrate before your crib, I believe you are the God of infinite Majesty, even though I see you here as a helpless babe. I humbly adore and thank you for having so humbled yourself for my salvation as to will to be born in a stable. I thank you for all you wished to suffer for me in Bethlehem, for your poverty and humility, for your nakedness, tears, cold and sufferings. Would that I could show you that tenderness which your Virgin Mother had toward you, and love you as she did. Would that I could praise you with the joy of the angels, that I could kneel before you with the faith of St. Joseph, the simplicity of the shepherds.

Uniting myself with these first adorers at the crib, I offer you the homage of my heart, and I beg that you would be born spiritually in my soul. Make me reflect in some degree the virtues of your admirable nativity. Fill me with that spirit of renunciation, of poverty, of humility, which prompted you to assume the weakness of our nature, and to be born amid destitution and suffering. Grant that from this day forward, I may in all things seek your greater glory, and may enjoy that peace promised to men of good will. Amen.

SILENT NIGHT *Franz Xaver Gruber and Joseph Mohr, 1818*
translated from German by John Freeman Young, 1859

Silent night, holy night,
All is calm, all is bright
Round yon virgin mother and child.
Holy infant, so tender and mild,
Sleep in heavenly peace,
Sleep in heavenly peace.

Silent night, holy night,
Shepherds quake at the sight;
Glories stream from heaven afar,
Heavenly hosts sing Alleluia!
Christ the Savior is born,
Christ the Savior is born!

Silent night, holy night,
Son of God, love's pure light;
Radiant beams from thy holy face
With the dawn of redeeming grace,
Jesus, Lord, at thy birth,
Jesus, Lord, at thy birth.

AWAY IN A MANGER *author unknown, late 19th century*
Away in a manger, no crib for a bed,
The little Lord Jesus laid down his sweet head.
The stars in the bright sky looked down where he lay,
The little Lord Jesus asleep on the hay.

The cattle are lowing, the baby awakes,
But little Lord Jesus, no crying he makes.
I love thee, Lord Jesus! look down from the sky,
And stay by my cradle till morning is nigh.

Be near me, Lord Jesus; I ask thee to stay
Close by me forever, and love me I pray.
Bless all the dear children in thy tender care,
And take us to heaven to live with thee there.

The Nativity of the Lord

DECEMBER 25TH SOLEMNITY/HOLYDAY OF OBLIGATION

COLLECT PRAYER

O God, who gladden us year by year as we wait in hope for our redemption grant that, just as we joyfully welcome your Only Begotten Son as our Redeemer, we may also merit to face him confidently when he comes again as our Judge. Who lives and reigns with you in the unity of the Holy Spirit, one God, for ever and ever. Amen.

BIBLE READING FOR THE FEAST *Luke 2:1-20*

In those days a decree went out from Caesar Augustus that the whole world should be enrolled. This was the first enrollment, when Quirinius was governor of Syria. So all went to be enrolled, each to his own town. And Joseph too went up from Galilee from the town of Nazareth to Judea, to the city of David that is called Bethlehem, because he was of the house and family of David, to be enrolled with Mary, his betrothed, who was with child. While they were there, the time came for her to have her child, and she gave birth to her firstborn son. She wrapped him in swaddling clothes and laid him in a manger, because there was no room for them in the inn.

Now there were shepherds in that region living in the fields and keeping the night watch over their flock. The angel of the Lord appeared to them and the glory of the Lord shone around them, and they were struck with great fear. The angel said to them, "Do not be afraid; for behold, I proclaim to you good news of great joy that will be for all the people. For today in the city of David a

continued

savior has been born for you who is Messiah and Lord. And this will be a sign for you: you will find an infant wrapped in swaddling clothes and lying in a manger." And suddenly there was a multitude of the heavenly host with the angel, praising God and saying:
 "Glory to God in the highest
 and on earth peace to those on whom his favor rests."

When the angels went away from them to heaven, the shepherds said to one another, "Let us go, then, to Bethlehem to see this thing that has taken place, which the Lord has made known to us." So they went in haste and found Mary and Joseph, and the infant lying in the manger. When they saw this, they made known the message that had been told them about this child. All who heard it were amazed by what had been told them by the shepherds. And Mary kept all these things, reflecting on them in her heart. Then the shepherds returned, glorifying and praising God for all they had heard and seen, just as it had been told to them.

An At Home Nativity Play

FROM LUKE 2:1-20 AND
MATTHEW 2:1-12

I created this script using Biblical text and familiar hymns, so that our whole family could really get to know the story, the people, and the actual words of the Nativity of Our Lord.

We use costumes from the dress up box and dad's closet, and sets and props from around the house.

Set up takes a half an hour to an hour, and the play takes about ten minutes.

The script can be used as a "table read" without sets, props, or costumes, but I'd recommend getting out your t-shirt turbans and doing the whole shebang.

There are eleven speaking roles. In smaller groups, individuals can play multiple roles. Bigger groups can add as many angels, shepherds, scribes, and wisemen as necessary.

If you've got a musician in the family, musical accompaniment is a plus, but acapella singing will do just fine.

No memorizing is required. The actors don't even have to be able to read. We choose a grown up to read the part of the narrator, and for our littlest actors, I'll just say their lines to them in a low voice, a line or two at a time, and they repeat them.

Two year olds to great-grandparents, extended family, out of town guests, and non Catholic friends have all participated in our little at home productions.

We've put on this play in our own home, on the evening of Christmas Day, for over ten years now. It's become a sweet, fun, often hilarious, and completely irreplaceable part of Christmas for us.

I hope your family will enjoy it as much as we have!

Cast of Characters

SPEAKING CHARACTERS:
Narrator
Joseph
Mary
1st Innkeeper
2nd Innkeeper
3rd Innkeeper
1st Angel
1st Shepherd
1st Wise man
Herod
Scribe

NON-SPEAKING CHARACTERS:
other angels (1 or more)
other shepherds (1 or more)
other wise men (2)
other scribes (0 or more)

CHORUS:
all actors and audience members

Costumes, props, and sets

SUGGESTIONS FOR COSTUMES:
Get out all of Dad's t-shirts, the more colors the better. Turn any with graphics inside out and give two to each actor, one for a tunic and one for a turban, veil, or head-scarf. Belt with ropes or bandanas or fabric scraps. Angels should have white shirts with paper wings stapled to the backs. Mary should be in blue. Herod needs a crown.

SUGGESTIONS FOR PROPS:
Mary should have a baby doll hidden under her dress. A stick horse or a rough cardboard cutout makes a great donkey. Shepherds can hold long sticks. Look around the house for containers for the gifts of the three wise men: perhaps a vase, a wooden box, and a metal bowl.

SUGGESTIONS FOR SETS:
Set up in the common room of your house. Try to un-clutter one side of the room and have the non-participants sit facing this way. For the stable you just need a roof of some sort. It could be a large piece of plywood or cardboard with one end on the floor and the other end resting on two chairs, or a sheet hung from the ceiling and pulled back and secured at the bottom with books or chairs to create a triangle space. It should have a large star hung above it. Decorate the stable area with stuffed animals and a cardboard box manger filled with a yellow or brown blanket or towel. Each innkeeper can hold up a piece of cardboard or a large (but not too heavy) book for Joseph to knock on.

ON·EARTH·PEACE·GOODWILL·TOWARDS·MEN.

The script

NARRATOR: And it came to pass, that in those days there went out a decree from Caesar Augustus, that the whole world should be enrolled. This enrolling was first made by Cyrinus, the governor of Syria. And all went to be enrolled, every one into his own city.

And Joseph also went up from Galilee, out of the city of Nazareth into Judea, to the city of David, which is called Bethlehem: because he was of the house and family of David, to be enrolled with Mary his espoused wife, who was with child.

Joseph leads Mary and the donkey from the back of the room.

JOSEPH: There it is Mary, we're almost there.

Joseph and Mary slowly walk around the room as the chorus sings.

CHORUS SINGS:
O little town of Bethlehem
How still we see thee lie
Above thy deep and dreamless sleep
The silent stars go by
Yet in thy dark streets shineth
The everlasting Light
The hopes and fears of all the years
Are met in thee tonight

JOSEPH: Now we'll find a place to stay for the night. Here's an inn.

They stop in front of the first door, Joseph knocks.

JOSEPH: Do you have any room for us?

The 1st innkeeper opens the door.

1ST INNKEEPER: Sorry, no room.

The 1st innkeeper closes the door. Joseph goes to the next door and knocks, the 2nd innkeeper opens the door.

JOSEPH: Do you have any room for us?

2ND INNKEEPER: Sorry, we're all full.

The 2nd innkeeper closes the door. Joseph goes to the next door and knocks. The 3rd innkeeper opens the door.

JOSEPH: Do you have any room for us?

3RD INNKEEPER: We're full too, I have no rooms to offer you, but I see that your wife is with child. Would you like to stay out back in the stable? It isn't much, but it will keep you out of the cold.

JOSEPH: Thank you, we will gladly take anything you can offer us.

Joseph and Mary walk to the stable.

MARY: I'm sure it will be fine, and I think we've arrived just in time.

NARRATOR: And it came to pass, that when they were there, her days were accomplished, that she should be delivered. And she brought forth her firstborn son, and wrapped him up in swaddling clothes, and laid him in a manger; because there was no room for them in the inn.

Mary removes the baby from her dress, wraps him in a blanket, and lays Him in the manger, then lays down next to Joseph to sleep.

CHORUS SINGS:
Away in a manger, no crib for a bed,
The little Lord Jesus laid down His sweet head.
The stars in the sky looked down where He lay,
The little Lord Jesus, asleep on the hay.

The shepherds stand in another part of the room.

NARRATOR: And there were in the same country shepherds watching, and keeping the night watches over their flock.

The angels walk up to them.

NARRATOR: And behold an angel of the Lord stood by them, and the brightness of God shone round about them; and they feared with a great fear. And the angel said to them:

1ST ANGEL: Fear not; for, behold, I bring you good tidings of great joy, that shall be to all the people: For, this day, is born to you a Saviour, who is Christ the Lord, in the city of David. And this shall be a sign unto you. You shall find the infant wrapped in swaddling clothes, and laid in a manger.

NARRATOR: And suddenly there was with the angel a multitude of the heavenly army, praising God, and saying:

ALL ANGELS: Glory to God in the highest; and on earth peace to men of good will.

CHORUS SINGS:
The First Noel, the Angels did say
Was to certain poor shepherds in fields as they lay
In fields where they lay keeping their sheep
On a cold winter's night that was so deep.
Noel, Noel, Noel, Noel Born is the King of Israel!

NARRATOR: And it came to pass, after the angels departed from them into heaven, the shepherds said one to another:

1ST SHEPHERD: Let us go over to Bethlehem, and let us see this word that is come to pass, which the Lord hath shewed to us.

The shepherds walk around the room, arriving at the stable at the end of the song and kneeling down before the manger. Joseph and Mary kneel down with them.

CHORUS SINGS:
O Come All Ye Faithful
Joyful and triumphant,
O come ye, O come ye to Bethlehem.
Come and behold Him,
Born the King of Angels;
O come, let us adore Him,
O come, let us adore Him,
O come, let us adore Him, Christ the Lord.

NARRATOR: And they came with haste; and they found Mary and Joseph, and the infant lying in the manger. And seeing, they understood of the word that had been spoken to them concerning this child. And all that heard, wondered; and at those things that were told them by the shepherds.

And the shepherds returned, glorifying and praising God, for all the things they had heard and seen, as it was told unto them.

The shepherds go sit down. Herod and his scribes stand in the front of the room, off to the side away from the stable. The 3 Wise men walk from the back of the room to the front.

NARRATOR: When Jesus therefore was born in Bethlehem of Juda, in the days of king Herod, behold, there came wise men from the east to Jerusalem. Saying,

1ST WISE MAN: Where is he that is born king of the Jews? For we have seen his star in the east, and are come to adore him.

NARRATOR: And king Herod hearing this, was troubled, and all Jerusalem with him. And assembling together all the chief priests and the scribes of the people, he inquired of them where Christ should be born. But they said to him:

SCRIBE: In Bethlehem of Juda. For so it is written by the prophet: And thou Bethlehem the land of Juda art not the least among the princes of Juda: for out of thee shall come forth the captain that shall rule my people Israel.

NARRATOR: Then Herod, privately calling the wise men, learned diligently of them the time of the star which appeared to them; And sending them into Bethlehem, said:

HEROD: Go and diligently inquire after the child, and when you have found him, bring me word again, that I also may come to adore him.

NARRATOR: After their audience with the king they set out.

The 3 Wise men walk slowly around the room, arriving at the stable at the end of the song.

CHORUS SINGS:
We three kings of Orient are
Bearing gifts we traverse afar
Field and fountain, moor and mountain
Following yonder star
O-o Star of wonder, star of night
Star with royal beauty bright
Westward leading, still proceeding
Guide us to thy Perfect Light

NARRATOR: Having heard the king, they went their way; and behold the star which they had seen in the east, went before them, until it came and stood over where the child was.

And seeing the star they rejoiced with exceeding great joy.

The 3 Kings give high-fives.

NARRATOR: And entering into the house, they found the child with Mary his mother, and falling down they adored him.

The 3 wise men kneel down before the manger.

NARRATOR: Opening their treasures, they offered him gifts; gold, frankincense, and myrrh.

Each wise man offers his gift to Mary in turn, then walk a little way away from the stable and lie down to sleep.

The angel comes and whispers in the ear of one wise man.

NARRATOR: And having received an answer in sleep that they should not return to Herod, they went back another way into their country.

The 3 wise men get up and go sit down.

Mary picks up the baby Jesus and rocks Him, with Joseph by her side.

NARRATOR: And Mary kept all these words, pondering them in her heart.

During the final song, all participants make their way up to the front of the room and take their bows.

CHORUS SINGS:
Joy to the world, the Lord is come!
Let earth receive her King;
Let every heart prepare Him room,
And Heaven and nature sing,
And Heaven and nature sing,
And Heaven, and Heaven, and nature sing.
Joy to the world, the Savior reigns!
Let men their songs employ;
While fields and floods, rocks, hills and plains
Repeat the sounding joy,
Repeat the sounding joy,
Repeat, repeat, the sounding joy.
He rules the world with truth and grace,
And makes the nations prove
The glories of His righteousness,
And wonders of His love,
And wonders of His love,
And wonders, wonders, of His love.

Saint Stephen

DECEMBER 26TH FEAST

COLLECT PRAYER
Grant, Lord, we pray, that we may imitate what we worship, and so learn to love even our enemies, for we celebrate the heavenly birthday of a man who know how to pray even for his persecutors. Through our Lord Jesus Christ, your Son, who lives and reigns with you in the unity of the Holy Spirit, one God, for ever and ever. Amen.

BIBLE READING FOR THE FEAST Acts 6:1-15, 7:51-60

At that time, as the number of disciples continued to grow, the Hellenists complained against the Hebrews because their widows were being neglected in the daily distribution. So the Twelve called together the community of the disciples and said, "It is not right for us to neglect the word of God to serve at table. Brothers, select from among you seven reputable men, filled with the Spirit and wisdom, whom we shall appoint to this task, whereas we shall devote ourselves to prayer and to the ministry of the word." The proposal was acceptable to the whole community, so they chose Stephen, a man filled with faith and the holy Spirit, also Philip, Prochorus, Nicanor, Timon, Parmenas, and Nicholas of Antioch, a convert to Judaism. They presented these men to the apostles who prayed and laid hands on them. The word of God continued to spread, and the number of the disciples in Jerusalem increased greatly; even a large group of priests were becoming obedient to the faith.

Now Stephen, filled with grace and power, was working great wonders and signs among the people. Certain members of the so-called Synagogue of Freedmen, Cyrenians, and Alexandrians, and people from Cilicia and Asia, came forward and debated with Stephen, but they could not withstand the wisdom and the spirit with which he spoke. Then they instigated some men to say,

continued

"We have heard him speaking blasphemous words against Moses and God." They stirred up the people, the elders, and the scribes, accosted him, seized him, and brought him before the Sanhedrin. They presented false witnesses who testified, "This man never stops saying things against this holy place and the law. For we have heard him claim that this Jesus the Nazorean will destroy this place and change the customs that Moses handed down to us." All those who sat in the Sanhedrin looked intently at him and saw that his face was like the face of an angel. . . .

"You stiff-necked people, uncircumcised in heart and ears, you always oppose the holy Spirit; you are just like your ancestors. Which of the prophets did your ancestors not persecute? They put to death those who foretold the coming of the righteous one, whose betrayers and murderers you have now become. You received the law as transmitted by angels, but you did not observe it."

When they heard this, they were infuriated, and they ground their teeth at him. But he, filled with the holy Spirit, looked up intently to heaven and saw the glory of God and Jesus standing at the right hand of God, and he said, "Behold, I see the heavens opened and the Son of Man standing at the right hand of God." But they

continued

cried out in a loud voice, covered their ears, and rushed upon him together. They threw him out of the city, and began to stone him. The witnesses laid down their cloaks at the feet of a young man named Saul. As they were stoning Stephen, he called out, "Lord Jesus, receive my spirit." Then he fell to his knees and cried out in a loud voice, "Lord, do not hold this sin against them"; and when he said this, he fell asleep.

A PRAYER FOR DEACONS AND OTHER MINISTERS
Heavenly Father,
since the time of the Apostles
you have inspired the Church
to commission certain members
to assist in a special way
in the pastoral mission of Christ.
Bless the deacons
and all other ordained
and non-ordained ministers
that they may be humble
and faith-inspired in their service.
We ask this through Christ, our Lord.
Amen.

GOOD KING WENCESLAS by John Mason Neale, 1853

Good King Wenceslas looked out
On the Feast of Stephen
When the snow lay round about
Deep and crisp and even
Brightly shone the moon that night
Though the frost was cruel
When a poor man came in sight
Gathering winter fuel

Hither, page, and stand by me,
If thou knowst it, telling
Yonder peasant, who is he?
Where and what his dwelling?
Sire, he lives a good league hence,
Underneath the mountain
Right against the forest fence
By Saint Agnes fountain.

Bring me flesh and bring me wine
Bring me pine logs hither
Thou and I shall see him dine
When we bear them thither.
Page and monarch, forth they went
Forth they went together
Through the rude winds wild lament
And the bitter weather

Sire, the night is darker now
And the wind blows stronger
Fails my heart, I know not how
I can go no longer.
Mark my footsteps, good my page
Tread thou in them boldly
Thou shall find the winters rage
Freeze thy blood less coldly.

In his masters step he trod
Where the snow lay dinted
Heat was in the very sod
Which the Saint had printed
Therefore, Christian men, be sure
Wealth or rank possessing
Ye, who now will bless the poor
Shall yourselves find blessing.

Saint John, Apostle & Evangelist

DECEMBER 27TH FEAST

COLLECT PRAYER

O God, who through the blessed Apostle John have unlocked for us the secrets of your Word, grant, we pray, that we may grasp with proper understanding what he has so marvelously brought to our ears. Through our Lord Jesus Christ, your Son, who lives and reigns with you in the unity of the Holy Spirit, one God, for ever and ever. Amen.

BIBLE READING FOR THE FEAST *Revelation 1:1-9*

The revelation of Jesus Christ, which God gave to him, to show his servants what must happen soon. He made it known by sending his angel to his servant John, who gives witness to the word of God and to the testimony of Jesus Christ by reporting what he saw. Blessed is the one who reads aloud and blessed are those who listen to this prophetic message and heed what is written in it, for the appointed time is near.

John, to the seven churches in Asia: grace to you and peace from him who is and who was and who is to come, and from the seven spirits before his throne, and from Jesus Christ, the faithful witness, the firstborn of the dead and ruler of the kings of the earth. To him who loves us and has freed us from our sins by his blood, who has made us into a kingdom, priests for his God and Father, to him be glory and power forever and ever. Amen.

Behold, he is coming amid the clouds,
    and every eye will see him,
    even those who pierced him.
All the peoples of the earth will lament him.
    Yes. Amen.

"I am the Alpha and the Omega," says the Lord God, "the one who is and who was and who is to come, the almighty."

ON SAINT PETER AND SAINT JOHN Homily of St. Augustine, excerpt

The Church recognizes two lives which Divinity himself has revealed and recommended. One is the life of faith, the other the life of vision; one the life of pilgrimage, the other life in the mansions of eternity; one the life of labor, the other the life of rest; one the life of the journey, the other the life of home; one the life of action, the other the life of contemplation. The one avoids evil and does good, the other knows no evil to avoid, but only a great good to enjoy. The one fights with the enemy, the other, having no enemy, reigns.

The one aids the needy, the other is where no needy are; the one forgives the trespasses of others that its own might be forgiven, the other has neither trespasses to forgive nor does anything which calls for forgiveness. The one is scourged with evils, lest it be made presumptuous by prosperity; the other possesses such a fullness of grace that it is without evil. Free from any temptation to pride, it adheres to the Supreme Good.

Wherefore one life is good, but as yet full of sorrows; the other is better, yea even blessed. The first is typified by the Apostle Peter, the other by John. The one life endures all labors up to the end of its alotted time, and there finds an end; the other, having fulfilled all things, stretches beyond the end of time, and in eternity finds no end. So, to Peter is said: "Follow me." Of the other, however; "If I wish him to remain until I come, what is that to thee? Follow thou me." What is the meaning of this? How much can I know of it? How much can I understand? What is it?--unless this: "You are to follow me, imitating me in suffering temporal evils.

Let him remain until I come, bringing eternal rewards."

Drinking the Love of Saint John

After blessing the wine, it is offered one to another as the love of Saint John. Using a single cup, passed from one person to the next, is traditional, but each person can use his own cup if the group prefers.

LEADER: Lord Jesus Christ, you did call yourself the vine and your holy Apostles the branches; and out of all those who love you, you desired to make a good vineyard. Bless this wine and pour into it the might of your benediction so that every one who drinks or takes of it, may through the intercession of your beloved disciple, the holy Apostle and Evangelist John, be freed from every disease or attack of illness and obtain health of body and soul.
Who lives and reigns forever.
ALL: Amen.

It may be sprinkled with holy water.

FIRST PERSON: I drink to you the love of St. John.
He takes a drink of wine.
SECOND PERSON: I thank you for the love of St. John.
He takes a drink of wine

The second person offers wine to the third. Repeat around the table until all have offered and received.

PRAYER TO SAINT JOHN
St. John, beloved disciple of Jesus, pray for us to be docile to those whom the Lord has put in authority over us, yet zealous in our love and service to God. In Jesus Christ's name, we pray. Amen.

Prayers for Priests

PRAYER FOR PRIESTS OF POPE BENEDICT XVI

Lord Jesus Christ, eternal High Priest,
You offered yourself to the Father on the altar of the Cross and through the outpouring of the Holy Spirit gave your priestly people a share in your redeeming sacrifice.
Hear our prayer for the sanctification of our priests. Grant that all who are ordained to the ministerial priesthood may be ever more conformed to you, the Divine Master.
May they preach the Gospel with pure heart and clear conscience.
Let them be shepherds according to your own Heart, single-minded in service to you and to the Church and shining examples of a holy, simple and joyful life.
Through the prayers of the Blessed Virgin Mary, your Mother and ours, draw all priests and the flocks entrusted to their care to the fullness of eternal life where you live and reign with the Father and the Holy Spirit, one God, forever and ever. Amen.

PRAYER FOR PRIESTS OF SAINT THERESE OF LISIEUX

O Jesus, I pray for your faithful and fervent priests;
for your unfaithful and tepid priests;
for your priests laboring at home or abroad in distant mission fields.
for your tempted priests;
for your lonely and desolate priests;
For your young priests; for your dying priests;
for the souls of your priests in Purgatory.
But above all, I recommend to you the priests dearest to me: the priest who baptized me;
the priests who absolved me from my sins;
the priests at whose Masses I assisted and who gave me your Body and Blood in Holy Communion;
the priests who taught and instructed me;
all the priests to whom I am indebted in any other way (especially *names here*).
O Jesus, keep them all close to your heart,
and bless them abundantly in time and in eternity. Amen.

The Holy Innocents

DECEMBER 28TH FEAST

COLLECT PRAYER
O God, whom the Holy Innocents confessed and proclaimed on this day, not by speaking but by dying, grant, we pray, that the faith in you which we confess with our lips may also speak through our manner of life. Through our Lord Jesus Christ, your Son, who lives and reigns with you in the unity of the Holy Spirit, one God, for ever and ever. Amen.

BIBLE READING FOR THE FEAST *Matthew 2:13-18*

When they had departed, behold, the angel of the Lord appeared to Joseph in a dream and said, "Rise, take the child and his mother, flee to Egypt, and stay there until I tell you. Herod is going to search for the child to destroy him." Joseph rose and took the child and his mother by night and departed for Egypt. He stayed there until the death of Herod, that what the Lord had said through the prophet might be fulfilled, "Out of Egypt I called my son.

When Herod realized that he had been deceived by the magi, he became furious. He ordered the massacre of all the boys in Bethlehem and its vicinity two years old and under, in accordance with the time he had ascertained

from the magi. Then was fulfilled what had been said through Jeremiah the prophet:

A voice was heard in Ramah, sobbing and loud lamentation;
Rachel weeping for her children, and she would not be consoled, since they were no more."

HOLY INNOCENTS PRAYER

We remember today, O God, the slaughter of the holy innocents of Bethlehem by King Herod. Receive, we pray, into the arms of your mercy all innocent victims; and by your great might frustrate the designs of evil tyrants and establish your rule of justice, love, and peace; through Jesus Christ our Lord, who lives and reigns with you and the Holy Spirit, one God, for ever and ever. Amen.

SAINT AUGUSTINE ON THE HOLY INNOCENTS

And while Herod thus persecutes Christ, he furnished an army of martyrs clothed in white robes of the same age as the Lord. Behold how this unrighteous enemy never could have so much profited these infants by his love as he did by his hate; for as much as iniquity abounded against them, so much did the grace of blessing abound on them. O blessed infants! He only will doubt of your crown in this your passion for Christ, who doubts that the baptism of Christ has a benefit for infants. He who at his birth had angels to proclaim him, the heavens to testify, and magi to worship him, could surely have prevented that these should not have died for him, had he not known that they died not in that death, but rather lived in higher bliss."

ALTAR SERVER'S PRAYER

Open my mouth, O Lord, to bless your Holy Name.
Cleanse my heart from all evil and distracting
 thoughts.
Enlighten my understanding and inflame my will that I
 may serve more worthily at your holy altar.
O Mary, Mother of Christ the High Priest, obtain for
 me the most important grace of knowing my
 vocation in life.
Grant me a true spirit of faith and humble obedience
 so that I may ever behold the priest as a
 representative of God and be willing to follow him in
 the Way, the Truth, and the Life of Christ. Amen.

COVENTRY CAROL by unknown, 16th century English carol
Lully, lullay, thou little tiny child,
bye, bye, lully lullay.

O sisters too, how may we do,
for to preserve this day,
this poor youngling for whom we sing,
bye, bye lully lullay.

Herod the king in his raging,
charged he hath this day,
his men of night, in his own sight,
all young children to slay.

Then woe is me, poor child, for thee!
And every morn and day,
for thy parting not say nor sing
bye, bye, lully lullay.

Lully, lullay, thou little tiny child,
bye, bye, lully lullay.

The Holy Family

SUNDAY AFTER CHRISTMAS OR DECEMBER 30TH SOLEMNITY/ HOLYDAY OF OBLIGATION

COLLECT PRAYER
O God, who were pleased to give us the shining example of the Holy Family, graciously grant that we may imitate them in practicing the virtues of family life and in the bonds of charity, and so, in the joy of your house, delight one day in eternal rewards. Through our Lord Jesus Christ, your Son, who lives and reigns with you in the unity of the Holy Spirit, one God, for ever and ever. Amen.

BIBLE READING FOR THE FEAST Luke 2:39-52
When they had fulfilled all the prescriptions of the law of the Lord, they returned to Galilee, to their own town of Nazareth. The child grew and became strong, filled with wisdom; and the favor of God was upon him.

Each year his parents went to Jerusalem for the feast of Passover, and when he was twelve years old, they went up according to festival custom. After they had completed its days, as they were returning, the boy Jesus remained behind in Jerusalem, but his parents did not know it. Thinking that he was in the caravan, they journeyed for a day and looked for him among their relatives and acquaintances, but not finding him, they returned to Jerusalem to look for him. After three days they found him in the temple, sitting in the midst of the teachers, listening to them and asking them questions, and all who heard him were astounded at his understanding and his answers. When his parents saw him, they were astonished, and his mother said to him, "Son, why have you done this to us? Your father and I have been looking for you with great anxiety." And he said to them, "Why were you looking for me? Did you not know that I must be in my Father's house?" But they did not understand what he said to them. He went down with them and came to Nazareth, and was obedient to them; and his mother kept all these things in her heart. And Jesus advanced in wisdom and age and favor before God and man.

PRAYER TO THE HOLY FAMILY *by Fr. F. X. Lasance, S.J.*
O most loving Jesus, who by your sublime and beautiful virtues of humility, obedience, poverty, modesty, charity, patience and gentleness, and by the example of your domestic life, did bless with peace and happiness the family you chose on earth, in your clemency look down upon this household, humbly prostrate before you and imploring your mercy.

Remember that this family belongs to you; for to you we have in a special way dedicated and devoted ourselves.

Look upon us in your loving kindness; preserve us from danger; give us help in time of need, and grant us the grace to persevere to the end in the imitation of your Holy Family; that having revered you and loved you faithfully on earth, we may bless and praise you eternally in heaven.

O Mary, most sweet Mother, to your intercession we have recourse, knowing that your Divine Son will hear your prayers.

And O glorious Patriarch, St. Joseph, assist us by your powerful mediation, and offer, by the hands of Mary, our prayers to Jesus. Amen.

Songs for Advent

COME THOU LONG EXPECTED JESUS by Charles Wesley, 1744
Come, thou long expected Jesus
Born to set thy people free;
From our fears and sins release us,
Let us find our rest in thee.
Israel's strength and consolation,
Hope of all the earth thou art;
Dear desire of every nation,
Joy of every longing heart.
Born thy people to deliver,
Born a child and yet a King,
Born to reign in us forever,
Now thy gracious kingdom bring.
By thine own eternal Spirit
Rule in all our hearts alone;
By thine all sufficient merit,
Raise us to thy glorious throne.

LO! HOW A ROSE E'ER BLOOMING 15th century German carol
Lo, how a Rose e'er blooming
From tender stem hath sprung!
Of Jesse's lineage coming,
As men of old have sung.
It came, a flow'ret bright,
Amid the cold of winter,
When half spent was the night.
Isaiah 'twas foretold it,
The Rose I have in mind;
With Mary we behold it,
The virgin mother kind.
To show God's love aright,
She bore to men a Savior,
When half spent was the night.
This Flow'r, whose fragrance tender
With sweetness fills the air,
Dispels with glorious splendor
The darkness everywhere.
True man, yet very God,
From sin and death he saves us,
And lightens every load.

O COME, O COME EMMANUEL

by unknown, 1861, and H. S. Coffin, 1916

1. O Come, thou Wisdom from on high,
And order all things mightily
To us the path of knowledge show
And teach us in her ways to go.

REFRAIN: Rejoice! Rejoice! Emmanuel
shall come to thee, O Israel.

2. O Come, O Come, thou Lord of might:
Who to thy tribes on Sinai's height
In Ancient times did give the law
In cloud, and majesty, and awe.
REFRAIN

3. O Come, thou rod of Jesse's stem,
From ev'ry foe deliver them
That trust Thy mighty power to save,
And give them victory o'er the grave.
REFRAIN

4. O Come, thou Key of David, come,
And open wide our heav'nly home,
Make safe the way that leads on high,
That we no more have cause to sigh.
REFRAIN

5. O Come, thou Dayspring from on High
And cheer us by thy drawing nigh.
Disperse the gloomy clouds of night
And death's dark shadow put to flight.
REFRAIN

6. O Come, Desire of nations, bind
In one the hearts of all mankind.
Bid every strife and quarrel cease
And fill the world with heaven's peace.
REFRAIN

7. O Come, O Come, Emmanuel,
And ransom captive Israel,
That mourns in lonely exile here
Until the Son of God appear.
REFRAIN

VENI, VENI EMMANUEL from *Psalteriolum Cantionum Catholicarum, 1710, and Cantiones Sacrae, 1878*

1. Veni, O Sapientia,
quae hic disponis omnia,
veni, viam prudentiae
ut doceas et gloriae.

REFRAIN: Gaude! Gaude! Emmanuel,
nascetur pro te Israel!

2. Veni, veni, Adonai,
qui populo in Sinai
legem dedisti vertice
in maiestate gloriae.
REFRAIN

3. Veni, O Iesse virgula,
ex hostis tuos ungula,
de specu tuos tartari
educ et antro barathri.
REFRAIN

4. Veni, Clavis Davidica,
regna reclude caelica,
fac iter tutum superum,
et claude vias inferum.
REFRAIN

5. Veni, veni O Oriens,
solare nos adveniens,
noctis depelle nebulas,
dirasque mortis tenebras.
REFRAIN

6. Veni, veni, Rex Gentium,
veni, Redemptor omnium,
ut salvas tuos famulos
peccati sibi conscios.
REFRAIN

7. Veni, veni, Emmanuel
captivum solve Israel,
qui gemit in exsilio,
privatus Dei Filio.
REFRAIN

CREATOR ALME SIDERUM by Pope Urban VIII, 1632
Creator alme siderum,
Aeterna lux credentium
Jesu Redemptor omnium,
Intende votis supplicum.

Qui daemonis ne fraudibus
Periret orbit, impetu
Amoris actus, languidi
Mundi medela factus es.

Commune qui mundi nefas
Ut expiares; ad crucem
E Virginis sacrario
Intacta prodis victima.

Cujus potestas gloriae,
Nomenque cum primum sonat
Et coelites et inferi
Tremente curvantur genu.

Te deprecamur ultimae
Magnum diei Judicem,
Armis supernae gratia;
Defende nos ab hostibus.

Virtus, honor, laus, gloria
Deo Patri cum Filio,
Sancto simul Paraclito,
In saeculorum saecula.

CREATOR OF THE STARS OF NIGHT *translated by John M. Neale, 1852*

Creator of the stars of night,
Thy people's everlasting light,
Jesu, Redeemer, save us all,
And hear Thy servants when they call.

Thou, grieving that the ancient curse
Should doom to death a universe,
Hast found the medicine, full of grace,
To save and heal a ruined race.

Thou cam'st, the Bridegroom of the bride,
As drew the world to evening-tide;
Proceeding from a virgin shrine,
The spotless victim all divine.

At whose dread name, majestic now,
All knees must bend, all hearts must bow;
And things celestial Thee shall own,
And things terrestrial, Lord alone.

O Thou whose coming is with dread
To judge and doom the quick and dead,
Preserve us, while we dwell below,
From every insult of the foe.

To God the Father, God the Son,
And God the Spirit, Three in One,
Laud, honor, might, and glory be
From age to age eternally.

O COME DIVINE MESSIAH
French Carol by Abbé Simon J. Pellegrin +1745, translated by Sister Mary of St. Philip

O come, divine Messiah!
The world in silence waits the day
When hope shall sing its triumph,
And sadness flee away.

REFRAIN: Dear Savior haste;
Come, come to earth,
Dispel the night and show your face,
And bid us hail the dawn of grace.

O come, divine Messiah!
The world in silence waits the day
When hope shall sing its triumph,
And sadness flee away. *REFRAIN*

O Christ, whom nations sigh for,
Whom priest and prophet long foretold,
Come break the captive fetters;
Redeem the long-lost fold. *REFRAIN*

You come in peace and meekness,
And lowly will your cradle be;
All clothed in human weakness
We shall your Godhead see. *REFRAIN*

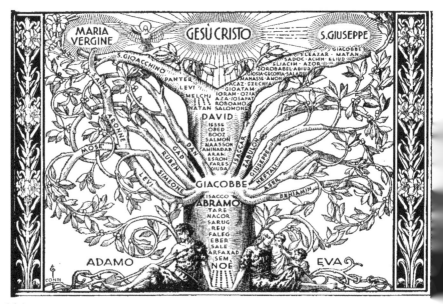

LET ALL MORTAL FLESH KEEP SILENCE from the Liturgy of St. James, 400; translated by Gerard Moultrie, 1864

Let all mortal flesh keep silence,
And with fear and trembling stand;
Ponder nothing earthly-minded,
For with blessing in his hand,
Christ our God to earth descended,
Our full homage to demand.

King of kings, yet born of Mary,
As of old on earth he stood,
Lord of lords, in human vesture,
In the body and the blood;
He will give to all the faithful
His own self for heav'nly food.

Rank on rank the host of heaven
Spreads its vanguard on the way,
As the Light of light descended
From the realms of endless day,
That the pow'rs of hell may vanish
As the darkness clears away.

At his feet the six-winged seraph,
Cherubim with sleepless eye,
Veil their faces to the presence,
As with ceaseless voice they cry:
"Alleluia, Alleluia,
Alleluia, Lord Most High!"

THE ANGEL GABRIEL FROM HEAVEN CAME *Basque Carol translated by Sabine Baring-Gould • 1924*

The angel Gabriel from Heaven came,
His wings as drifted snow, his eyes as flame;
All hail, said he, thou lowly maiden Mary,
Most highly favored lady, Gloria!

For know a blessèd mother thou shalt be,
All generations laud and honor thee,
Thy Son shall be Emmanuel, by seers foretold,
Most highly favored lady, Gloria!

Then gentle Mary meekly bowed her head,
To me be as it pleaseth God, she said,
My soul shall laud and magnify his holy name.
Most highly favored lady, Gloria!

Of her, Emmanuel, the Christ, was born
In Bethlehem, all on a Christmas morn,
And Christian folk throughout the world will ever say—
Most highly favored lady, Gloria!

PEOPLE LOOK EAST *Eleanor Farjeon, 1928*

People, look east. The time is near
Of the crowning of the year.
Make your house fair as you are able,
Trim the hearth and set the table.
People, look east and sing today:
Love, the guest, is on the way.

Furrows, be glad. Though earth is bare,
One more seed is planted there:
Give up your strength the seed to nourish,
That in course the flower may flourish.
People, look east and sing today:
Love, the rose, is on the way.

Birds, though you long have ceased to build,
Guard the nest that must be filled.
Even the hour when wings are frozen
God for fledging time has chosen.
People, look east and sing today:
Love, the bird, is on the way.

Stars, keep the watch. When night is dim
One more light the bowl shall brim,
Shining beyond the frosty weather,
Bright as sun and moon together.
People, look east and sing today:
Love, the star, is on the way.

Angels, announce with shouts of mirth
Christ who brings new life to earth.
Set every peak and valley humming
With the word, the Lord is coming.
People, look east and sing today:
Love, the Lord, is on the way.

I'LL BE HOME FOR CHRISTMAS Kim Gannon and Walter Kent, 1943

I'll be home for Christmas
You can plan on me
Please have snow and mistletoe
And presents on the tree
Christmas Eve will find me
Where the love light gleams
I'll be home for Christmas
If only in my dreams

I'll be home for Christmas
You can plan on me
Please have snow and mistletoe
And presents on the tree
Christmas Eve'll find me
Where the love light gleams
I'll be home for Christmas
If only in my dreams

CHRISTMAS IS COMING

from a traditional nursery rhyme, frequently sung as a round

Christmas is coming, the goose is getting fat
Please put a penny in the old man's hat
If you haven't got a penny, a ha'penny will do
If you haven't got a ha'penny, then God bless you!

SILVER BELLS *Jay Livingston and Ray Evans, 1950*

Silver bells, silver bells
It's Christmas time in the city
Ring-a-ling, hear them ring
Soon it will be Christmas day

City sidewalks, busy sidewalks
Dressed in holiday style
In the air there's a feeling of Christmas
Children laughing, people passing
Meeting smile after smile
And on every street corner you hear

Silver bells, silver bells
It's Christmas time in the city
Ring-a-ling,
Hear them ring,
Soon it will be Christmas day

Strings of street lights, even stoplights
Blinkin' bright red and green
As the shoppers rush home with their treasures
Hear the snow crunch, see the kids bunch
This is Santa's big day
And above all this bustle you hear

Silver bells, silver bells
It's Christmas time in the city
Ring-a-ling,
Hear them ring,
Soon it will be Christmas day

City sidewalks, busy sidewalks
Dressed in holiday style
In the air there's a feeling of Christmas
Children laughing, people passing
Meeting smile after smile
Very soon it will be Christmas day

SANTA CLAUS IS COMING TO TOWN

John Frederick Coots and Haven Gillespie 1934

You better watch out
You better not cry
Better not pout
I'm telling you why
Santa Claus is coming to town
He's making a list
And checking it twice;
Gonna find out who's naughty and nice
Santa Claus is coming to town

He sees you when you're sleeping
He knows when you're awake
He knows if you've been bad or good
So be good for goodness sake!
O! You better watch out!
You better not cry
Better not pout
I'm telling you why
Santa Claus is coming
Santa Claus is coming
Santa Claus is coming to town

DECK THE HALLS *from a Welsh carol, 16th century*
Deck the halls with boughs of holly, Fa la la la la la la la!

'Tis the season to be jolly, Fa la la la la la la la!
Don we now our gay apparel, Fa la la la la la la la!
Troll the ancient Yuletide carol, Fa la la la la la la la!

See the blazing yule before us, Fa la la la la la la la!
Strike the harp and join the chorus, Fa la la la la la la la!

Follow me in merry measure, Fa la la la la la la la!
While I tell of Yuletide treasure, Fa la la la la la la la!

Fast away the old year passes, Fa la la la la la la la!
Hail the new, ye lads and lasses, Fa la la la la la la la!
Sing we joyous all together! Fa la la la la la la la!
Heedless of the wind and weather, Fa la la la la la la la!

JINGLE BELLS *by James Lord Pierpont, 1857*
Dashing through the snow
In a one-horse open sleigh
O'er the fields we go
Laughing all the way

Bells on bob tail ring
Making spirits bright
What fun it is to ride and sing
A sleighing song tonight!

Jingle bells, jingle bells,
Jingle all the way.
Oh! what fun it is to ride
In a one-horse open sleigh. *(repeat)*

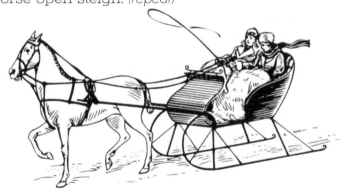

Songs for Christmas

I SAW THREE SHIPS COME SAILING IN by unknown, 17th century

I saw three ships come sailing in,
   On Christmas day, on Christmas day,
I saw three ships come sailing in,
   On Christmas day in the morning.

And what was in those ships all three?
   On Christmas day, on Christmas day,
And what was in those ships all three?
   On Christmas day in the morning.

Our Saviour Christ and his lady
   On Christmas day, on Christmas day,
Our Saviour Christ and his lady,
   On Christmas day in the morning.

Pray whither sailed those ships all three?
   On Christmas day, on Christmas day,
Pray whither sailed those ships all three?
   On Christmas day in the morning.

Oh, they sailed into Bethlehem,
   On Christmas day, on Christmas day,
Oh, they sailed into Bethlehem,
   On Christmas day in the morning.

And all the bells on earth shall ring,
   On Christmas day, on Christmas day,
And all the bells on earth shall ring,
   On Christmas day in the morning.

And all the Angels in heaven shall sing,
   On Christmas day, on Christmas day,
And all the Angels in heaven shall sing,
   On Christmas day in the morning.

And all the souls on earth shall sing,
   On Christmas day, on Christmas day,
And all the souls on earth shall sing,
   On Christmas day in the morning.
Then let us all rejoice, again,
   On Christmas day, on Christmas day,
Then let us all rejoice, again,
   On Christmas day in the morning.

CHILDREN, GO WHERE I SEND THEE

traditional African-American spiritual song

Children go where I send thee,
How shall I send thee?
I'm gonna send thee
One by one
One for the little, bitty baby
Born, born, born in Bethlehem.

Children go where I send thee,
How shall I send thee?
I'm gonna send thee
Two by two
Two for Paul and Silas
One for the little, bitty baby
Born, born, born in Bethlehem.

Children go where I send thee,
How shall I send thee?
I'm gonna send thee
Three by three
Three for the Hebrew children
Two for Paul and Silas
One for the little, bitty baby
Born, born, born in Bethlehem.

Children go where I send thee,
How shall I send thee?
I'm gonna send thee
Four by four
Four for the four that stood at the door.
Three for the Hebrew children
Two for Paul and Silas
One for the little, bitty baby
Born, born, born in Bethlehem.

ANGELS WE HAVE HEARD ON HIGH
from a French carol, translated by James Chadwick, 1862

Angels we have heard on high
Sweetly singing o'er the plains
And the mountains in reply
Echoing their joyous strains
Gloria in excelsis Deo!
Gloria in excelsis Deo!

Shepherds, why this jubilee?
Why your joyous strains prolong?
What the gladsome tidings be?
Which inspire your heavenly songs?
Gloria in excelsis Deo!
Gloria in excelsis Deo!

Come to Bethlehem and see
Him whose birth the angels sing;
Come, adore on bended knee,
Christ the Lord, the newborn King.
Gloria in excelsis Deo!
Gloria in excelsis Deo!

See Him in a manger laid,
Jesus, Lord of heaven and earth;
Mary, Joseph, lend your aid,
With us sing our Saviour's birth.
Gloria in excelsis Deo!
Gloria in excelsis Deo!

WHAT CHILD IS THIS? *by William Chatterton Dix, 1865*
What Child is this, who, laid to rest,
On Mary's lap is sleeping?
Whom angels greet with anthems sweet,
While shepherds watch are keeping?

REFRAIN: This, this is Christ, the King,
Whom shepherds guard and angels sing:
Haste, haste to bring him laud,
The Babe, the Son of Mary!

Why lies he in such mean estate,
Where ox and ass are feeding?
Good Christian, fear: for sinners here
The silent Word is pleading. *REFRAIN*

So bring him incense, gold, and myrrh,
Come, peasant, king to own him.
The King of kings salvation brings;
Let loving hearts enthrone him. *REFRAIN*

JOY TO THE WORLD *by Isaac Watts, 1719*
Joy to the World; the Lord is come!
Let earth receive her King!
Let ev'ry heart prepare him room,
And heaven and nature sing,
and heaven and nature sing,
and heaven and heaven and nature sing.

Joy to the earth, the Savior reigns!
Let men their songs employ;
While fields & floods, rocks, hills
   & plains
Repeat the sounding joy,
repeat the sounding joy,
repeat, repeat the sounding joy.

He rules the world with truth
   and grace,
And makes the nations prove
The glories of his
   righteousness,
And wonders of his love,
and wonders of his love,
and wonders, wonders, of his love.

HARK, THE HERALD ANGELS SING

from a hymn by Charles Wesley, 1739

Hark! the herald angels sing
"Glory to the newborn King
Peace on earth and mercy mild,
God and sinners reconciled!"
Joyful, all ye nations rise;
Join the triumph of the skies;
With angelic host proclaim
"Christ is born in Bethlehem!"
Hark! the herald angels sing
"Glory to the newborn King!"

Christ, by highest heaven adored;
Christ the everlasting Lord;
Late in time behold him come,
Offspring of the favored one.
Veiled in flesh, the Godhead see;
Hail the incarnate Deity
Pleased as man with men to dwell,
Jesus, our Emmanuel
Hark! the herald angels sing,
"Glory to the newborn King"

Hail! the heaven-born Prince of Peace!
Hail! the Son of Righteousness!
Light and life to all He brings,
Risen with healing in His wings.
Mild He lays His glory by,
Born that man no more may die;
Born to raise the sons of earth,
Born to give them second birth
Hark! the herald angels sing,
"Glory to the newborn King"

O COME ALL YE FAITHFUL
by unknown, translated by Fr. Frederick Oakeley, 1841

O come, all ye faithful, joyful and triumphant!
O come ye, O come ye to Bethlehem;
Come and behold him
Born the King of Angels:
O come, let us adore him, (3×)
Christ the Lord.

Sing, choirs of angels, sing in exultation,
Sing, all ye citizens of heaven above!
Glory to God, glory in the highest:
O come, let us adore him, (3×)
Christ the Lord.

Yea, Lord, we greet thee,
born this happy morning;
Jesus, to thee be glory given!
Word of the Father,
now in flesh appearing!
O come, let us adore him, (3×)
Christ the Lord.

ADESTE FIDELES
Adeste fideles læti triumphantes,
Venite, venite in Bethlehem.
Natum videte
Regem angelorum:
Venite adoremus (3×)
Dominum.

Cantet nunc io, chorus angelorum;
Cantet nunc aula cælestium,
Gloria, gloria in excelsis Deo,
Venite adoremus (3×)
Dominum.

Ergo qui natus die hodierna,
Jesu, tibi sit gloria,
Patris æterni Verbum caro factum,
Venite adoremus (3×)
Dominum.

O LITTLE TOWN OF BETHLEHEM by Philips Brooks 1868
O little town of Bethlehem,
how still we see thee lie!
Above thy deep and dreamless sleep
the silent stars go by.
Yet in thy dark streets shineth
the everlasting light;
the hopes and fears of all the years
are met in thee tonight.

For Christ is born of Mary
and, gathered all above,
while mortals sleep, the angels keep
their watch of wond'ring love.
O morning stars, together
proclaim the holy birth,
and praises sing to God the King,
and peace to men on earth.

How silently, how silently
the wondrous gift is giv'n!
So God imparts to human hearts
the blessings of His heav'n.
No ear may hear His coming,
but in this world of sin,
where meek souls will receive him still
the dear Christ enters in.

THE FIRST NOEL by Unknown, 16th Century
The First Noel, the Angels did say
Was to certain poor shepherds in fields as they lay
In fields where they lay keeping their sheep
On a cold winter's night that was so deep.
REFRAIN: Noel, Noel, Noel, Noel
Born is the King of Israel!

They looked up and saw a star
Shining in the East beyond them far
And to the earth it gave great light
And so it continued both day and night. REFRAIN

And by the light of that same star
Three Wise men came from country far
To seek for a King was their intent
And to follow the star wherever it went. REFRAIN

GOD REST YE MERRY GENTLEMEN by unknown, 16th century
God rest ye merry gentlemen
Let nothing you dismay
Remember Christ our Savior
Was born on Christmas Day
To save us all from Satan's pow'r
When we were gone astray

REFRAIN: Oh tidings of comfort and joy
Comfort and joy, oh tidings of comfort and joy

In Bethlehem, in Juda
This blessed Babe was born
And laid within a manger
Upon this blessed morn
The which his Mother Mary
Did nothing take in scorn REFRAIN

From God our Heavenly Father
A blessed Angel came
And unto certain shepherds
Brought tidings of the same
How that in Bethlehem was born
The Son of God by name REFRAIN

Fear not, then, said the angel,
Let nothing you affright;
This day is born a Savior
Of a pure virgin bright,
To free all those who trust in him
From Satan's power and might REFRAIN

WE WISH YOU A MERRY CHRISTMAS by unknown, 19th century
We wish you a Merry Christmas, we wish you a Merry Christmas, we wish you a Merry Christmas, and a Happy New Year.

REFRAIN: Good tidings we bring for you and your kin, Good tidings for Christmas and a Happy New Year.

Oh bring us some figgy pudding (x3)
and bring it right here. REFRAIN

We won't go until we get some (x3)
so bring some out here. REFRAIN

WE THREE KINGS *by Rev. John Henry Hopkins, 1857*
We three kings of Orient are
Bearing gifts we traverse afar
Field and fountain, moor and mountain
Following yonder star

REFRAIN: O-o Star of wonder, star of night
Star with royal beauty bright
Westward leading, still proceeding
Guide us to thy Perfect Light

Born a King on Bethlehem's plain
Gold I bring to crown him again
King forever, ceasing never
Over us all to reign *REFRAIN*

Frankincense to offer have I
Incense owns a Deity nigh
Prayer and praising, all men raising
Worship him, God most high *REFRAIN*

Myrrh is mine, its bitter perfume
Breathes of life of gathering gloom
Sorrowing, sighing, bleeding, dying
Sealed in the stone-cold tomb *REFRAIN*

Glorious now behold him arise
King and God and Sacrifice
Alleluia, Alleluia
Earth to heav'n replies *REFRAIN*

THE TWELVE DAYS OF CHRISTMAS

from a French carol, translated by Frederic Austin, 1909

December 25: On the first day of Christmas, my true love gave to me a partridge in a pear tree.

December 26: On the second day of Christmas my true love gave to me two turtle doves and a partridge in a pear tree.

December 27: On the third day of Christmas my true love gave to me three French hens, two turtle doves and a partridge in a pear tree.

December 28: On the fourth day of Christmas my true love gave to me four calling birds, three French hens, two turtle doves and a partridge in a pear tree.

December 29: On the fifth day of Christmas my true love gave to me five golden rings, four calling birds, three French hens, two turtle doves and a partridge in a pear tree.

December 30: On the sixth day of Christmas my true love gave to me six geese a-laying, five golden rings, four calling birds, three French hens, two turtle doves and a partridge in a pear tree.

December 26: On the seventh day of Christmas my true love gave to me seven swans a-swimming, six geese a-laying, five golden rings, four calling birds, three French hens, two turtle doves and a partridge in a pear tree.

January 1: On the eighth day of Christmas my true love gave to me eight maids a-milking, seven swans a-swimming, six geese a-laying, five golden rings, four calling birds, three French hens, two turtle doves and a partridge in a pear tree.

January 3: On the ninth day of Christmas my true love gave to me nine ladies dancing, eight maids a-milking, seven swans a-swimming, six geese a-laying, five golden rings, four calling birds, three French hens, two turtle doves and a partridge in a pear tree.

January 4: On the tenth day of Christmas my true love gave to me ten lords a-leaping, nine ladies dancing, eight maids a-milking, seven swans a-swimming, six geese a-laying, five golden rings, four calling birds, three French hens, two turtle doves and a partridge in a pear tree.

January 5: On the eleventh day of Christmas my true love gave to me eleven pipers piping, ten lords a-leaping, nine ladies dancing, eight maids a-milking, seven swans a-swimming, six geese a-laying, five golden rings, four calling birds, three French hens, two turtle doves and a partridge in a pear tree.

January 6: On the twelfth day of Christmas my true love gave to me twelve drummers drumming, eleven pipers piping, ten lords a-leaping, nine ladies dancing, eight maids a-milking, seven swans a- swimming, six geese a-laying, five golden rings, four calling birds, three French hens, two turtle doves and a partridge in a pear tree.

Made in the USA
Monee, IL
19 November 2020